Macroeconomics in Times of Liquidity Crises

The Ohlin Lectures

See http://mitpress.mit.edu for a complete list of titles in this series.

Macroeconomics in Times of Liquidity Crises

Searching for Economic Essentials

Guillermo Calvo

The MIT Press
Cambridge, Massachusetts
London, England

This book was set in Palation by Toppan Best-set Premedia Limited. Printed and bound in the United States of America.

Library of Congress Cataloging-in-Publication Data

Names: Calvo, Guillermo A., author.
Title: Macroeconomics in times of liquidity crises : searching for economic essentials / Guillermo A. Calvo.
Description: Cambridge, MA : MIT Press, 2016. | Series: The Ohlin lectures | Includes bibliographical references and index.
Identifiers: LCCN 2016016503 | ISBN 9780262035415 (hardcover : alk. paper)
Subjects: LCSH: Liquidity (Economics) | Financial crises. | Money. | Macroeconomics.
Classification: LCC HG178 .C35 2016 | DDC 339--dc23 LC record available at https://lccn.loc.gov/2016016503

10 9 8 7 6 5 4 3 2 1

In grateful memory of Professor Julio H. G. Olivera, who motivated and inspired generations of Argentine economists

Contents

Preface

When I got the email from Mats Lundahl on December 2011 inviting me to give the Ohlin lectures, I was elated. The Heckscher–Ohlin–Samuelson theorem was one of my first encounters with economics. It left an indelible mark on my mind and set the roots for a long-lasting love for economics. The theorem has three features that appealed to me: simplicity, potential relevance, and beauty. A few minutes after reading the email, though, elation gave rise to a creepy feeling of inadequacy. I have spent most of my career working on macroeconomics. International trade was not absent from my catalog, but there was hardly anything that I could readily offer, and that I would consider fitting for honoring the memory of someone who had made seminal contributions to the field. I shared my trepidations with Mats and my dear friend Ron Findlay, who quickly, but gently, disabused me of my wrong priors. Actually, Professor Ohlin's wings have covered a wide spectrum of other issues, among which there exists a large number of newspaper columns on the Great Depression written in Swedish while the crisis was taking place (which, fortunately, are summarized in Carlson and Jonung 2002). Thus, all of a sudden, clouds parted, and contact with the great man was established. I immediately replied to Mats with a resounding "yes"!

Visiting the Stockholm School of Economics was a treat. Mats officiated as an accomplished chaperone. My wife Sara and I enjoyed every minute of it, and we had the privilege of meeting some of Professor Ohlin's family. As we were leaving the Stockholm's airport, I felt inspired and ready to start writing this book, but it did not take long for me to realize that there was a long distance between the lectures and the keyboard. In the lectures I was able to combine experience, intuition, and a little bit of theory—and convey my view about the recent financial crises, putting special emphasis on emerging market economies, which had first exposed me to the mysterious ways in which these crises evolve. I realized afterward that the glue that helped me to feel comfortable about these various issues contained a large dosage of *emotion*—not a sentiment that is highly regarded by my peers! Thus my first attempts at writing this book resulted, not in a cohesive oeuvre, but in a series of essays full of duplication and little "soul." Besides, while I was struggling to find the *right* approach for the book, a torrent of books and papers started to circulate, not to speak of the torrent of relevant factual information that was filtering in nonstop every day! Keeping up with the literature and events militated against finding the soul of the book. "Soul," as is well known, can only be found by introspection.

It eventually dawned on me that I had to "swim or sink," and that perhaps the best way to serve the reader was to offer a coherent view that abstracted from many details, important as they were, and concentrated on "essentials." This is captured in the book's subtitle. Then again, the title highlights two interrelated themes in the book: (1) liquidity crises and (2) the resulting crisis of macroeconomics. This focus, incidentally, gave further relevance to the search for essentials. Facing a debacle it is wise to take a look at the big picture, trees can wait![1] Admittedly, however, the picture examined in the book, although large for economics standards, is confined to issues that arise mostly in economists' circles. There is no effort made to bring to the discussion insights from other disciplines like psychology, anthropology, or history. These insights are important, but the book argues that substantial progress can be made by expanding the focus of traditional macro models to account for liquidity considerations.

The first task in writing the book was to find a center of gravity: one or two concepts that help give coherence to the conceptual discussion, and around which the rest of the book's universe rotate. In this respect I try to convince the reader that "liquidity" and "liquidity crunch" are phenomena around which many of the other facets of crisis episodes rotate. Relatedly, I resuscitate a fundamental idea hidden in Keynes's *General Theory* that has gone unnoticed in mainstream macroeconomics (and Keynes himself does not seem to have done much with it), namely that the resilience of currencies like the US dollar may have a lot to do with these currencies' role as worldwide units of account and, more important, to the prevalence of *nominal rigidities*. Conventional theory portrays nominal rigidities as the bane for full employment. However, Keynes's conjecture, which I label "The Price Theory of Money," suggests that nominal rigidities are the rock on which paper monies anchor their flimsy feet on real output. This helps rationalize the incredible resilience of the US dollar, for instance, while other dollar-denominated assets that, in principle, should enjoy a stronger output backing suffered a devastating liquidity crunch. These ideas lie at the core of the book or, perhaps, I should say at its "soul." The rest of the book elaborates on the limbs that connect the soul with stylized facts associated with financial crises—both in emerging and developed economies—and with conventional and recent macro theory.[2]

Another reason for highlighting "liquidity" factors is that major recent financial crises are *systemic*, in the sense that they occur simultaneously in a variety of different economies. Idiosyncratic factors are no doubt important, but given the ubiquity of systemic crises, the first step should be to identify phenomena that can hit economies displaying widely different "fundamentals" at about the same time.[3] Thinking long and hard about this issue led me to zero in on the payments system for which liquid assets are of essence. Individual economies' vulnerabilities are not enough to rationalize systemic crises. This is important to keep in mind because the simultaneity of financial crises is not a popular topic in current theory. This worries me because ignoring systemic crises may drive us to focus on old "fundamentals," such as productivity shocks, in which the global payments system plays no significant role.

The audience that I have in mind for the book are individuals who are already familiar with the large popular literature summarizing the many details of financial crises, but have reached a point where the need for substance overtakes the thrill of anecdote—and are interested in getting a more in-depth or, if you will, *essential* view of these issues. Chapters 1, 2, and 6, and the introduction to part II offer this in plain English. The discussion in the rest of the book is more aimed at my peers—and hence requires some training in economics. However, most of the chapters are spiced up with enough comments that should help the reader grasp the main intuitions without having to work through formal derivations.

The book puts global liquidity shocks at center stage, but it does not offer a framework that helps "predict" the next crisis—for example, it does not attempt to push the frontier of "leading indicators." As a first approximation, global shocks are taken as exogenous. Instead, the book will elaborate on (1) facts that show the importance of liquidity shocks, (2) resilience of some liquid assets to liquidity shocks, (3) the limits of standard monetary policy during a liquidity crisis, and (4) domestic factors that may exacerbate the depth of global liquidity shocks on output and the labor market, and the speed of recovery. The book therefore does not attempt to offer a new "General Theory" but rather highlights some factors and mechanisms that are useful and occasionally insightful in understanding the whole picture. Neither does the book attempt to give a survey of the financial crisis literature, so I must apologize for the lack of a comprehensive relevant bibliography. The book is based on my Ohlin lectures in which the objective was to offer a unified, but simple, view of financial crises, with special emphasis in emerging market economies.

There is something that I should like to make very clear. I strained to make the book highly readable and to keep the technicalities as simple as possible. But my own personal motivation is to search for "economic essentials." Essentials modern economics tends to disregard and privilege instead extensions of mainstream models. I hasten to say that I would be the last one not to appreciate sophisticated models. However, I am afraid that some of my peers will tend to take a discussion of some of the "essentials" discussed in this book as an attempt to inform the layman or the undergraduate student, but having scant value for them. I beg to disagree. In fact I think the liquidity discussion in the book has some novel insights for the modern economist (although I am less sure these insights would be considered novel by the likes of Keynes, Fischer, or Minsky!) that could help solidify the foundations of macroeconomic analysis, particularly in regard to financial crises. Hopefully, then, if my somewhat immodest claims contain some truth, the book could also serve as inspiration for the architects and designers in the profession, especially those prepared to think "out of the box."

In writing a book of this nature, one tends to incur many debts, and the present instance is no exemption. I will not attempt to list the names of all to whom I am highly indebted because the list will be a "who's who," and I am likely to leave out names that I will later regret. So I will mention, without implicating, the names of just a few with whom I have spent many hours and days puzzling over the issues raised in this book: Fabrizio Coricelli, Alejandro Izquierdo, Enrique Mendoza, Pablo Ottonello, Carmen Reinhart, Ernesto Talvi, Carlos Végh, and Andrés Velasco. Last, but not least, I would like to thank Sara Calvo for her selfless support and penetrating comments and insights—constantly and during many years.

The book has also greatly benefited by constructive (and occasionally acrimonious) comments from several anonymous referees, as well as MIT's editorial help and encouragement during a long journey. I am especially indebted to Jane Macdonald, Acquisitions Editor at MIT Press.

Introduction

As the ravages of the subprime crisis that started in 2007 and became fully evident in 2008 are sinking into the collective conscience, the self-assertiveness that dominated the developed market economies (DMs) is fading away, and giving rise to a nagging sense of insecurity. Prior to 2007, financial crisis episodes in emerging market economies (EMs) had already shown that both saints and sinners could be casualties. The Asian Tigers, the paragon of good macro policy, suffered major setbacks in 1997, a crisis that was followed by an even more disconcerting one: the Russian 1998 crisis, which spread its wings all across the EM landscape. Nonetheless, these episodes were discounted by DMs under the presupposition that their economies had much stronger financial institutions and the fact that they had enjoyed a high degree of macroeconomic stability since the 1980s (which included a period called the *Great Moderation*).

That was then. The subprime crisis that started in 2007 has changed economists' views in a radical way. There is now no major disagreement that a key source of trouble in the current episode is the financial sector's dysfunctionality, possibly induced by populist policies and institutions such as Fannie

Mae (e.g., see Calomiris 2009). As the narrative goes, financial excesses were eventually revealed by problems in the subprime mortgages' market, which gave rise to a massive *liquidity* crisis and a *flight to quality*—the latter taking the form of excess demand for "hard currencies" (also called *safe currencies* in this book), a phenomenon that is usually labeled *liquidity trap*.[1] These concepts are only now being subject to rigorous analysis.

Interestingly, however, liquidity crunch and liquidity trap are, in principle, mutually incompatible phenomena, a fact that seems to have escaped economists' attention. Liquidity crunch takes place because the market fears that some key liquid financial assets (e.g., asset-backed securities, ABS) will become less acceptable as Means of Exchange (MOE) or credit collateral. Liquidity trap is a situation in which the public reveals an insatiable appetite for, typically, some safe fiat money (e.g., US dollar or yen). The puzzle is that fiat monies are assumed in the literature to have a weaker output backup than, say, ABS. Thus the question arises, why would investors fly away from ABS and into US dollar, for example? This basic question calls for an answer.

Fortunately, Keynes's *General Theory* has an answer that, curiously, appears to have been totally overlooked by the profession. The answer could be paraphrased in Clinton-esque lingo as: *It is sticky wages/prices, stupid!* According to this view, which I will label the Price Theory of Money (PTM), fiat money is backed up in real terms by the *inflexibility* of prices and wages (accompanied by some flexibility in the supply of output and labor services at given prices).[2] Under these circumstances, wage earners and firms become, in a fashion, the lenders of last resort for fiat money. This feature gives to money a *stable* output backup not available for most other financial assets (except bank deposits and other assets ensured by the corresponding central bank or lender of last resort), and it helps explain why a run on financial assets could be consistent with liquidity trap—and why, under normal conditions, monetary economies in a multi-monies world are more stable than the existence of flimsy fiat monies would lead us to believe. As I will argue, the PTM offers some solid ground to justify the relative resiliency of the output value of money and the pyramid of financial assets that are denominated in terms of money (especially bonds). The PTM rationalization for the value of money is radically different from standard explanations based on regulations like legal tender and the obligation to pay taxes with domestic money instruments. The mechanism behind the PTM could conceivably be spontaneously generated by the private sector and have ramification that go far beyond the confines of individual countries (as is the case of reserve currencies, i.e., currencies that are employed in international transactions). It is therefore a theory that is especially adept to addressing global liquidity issues encountered in systemic financial crises.

The book will be centered on the assumption that liquidity crunch is the main triggering factor behind financial crises. The reason for taking liquidity crunch as a largely exogenous shock is that there is a well-established microeconomic literature showing that "liquidity" is a fragile object subject to "runs," and that the latter may result in the economy permanently shifting to *another* equilibrium (see the seminal paper by Diamond and Dybvig 1983). The Diamond–Dybvig approach to liquidity runs helps rationalize the fact that major financial crises have an important "surprise" component expressed in the unusually large size and the hard to predict timing of these crises. Moreover this approach comes with an important bonus: it greatly simplifies the discussion and hence offers a reliable "first approximation."[3]

A sharp focus on liquidity allows highlighting some characteristics of liquid assets that are easy to miss otherwise. For example, as I argue in the book, the set of liquid assets may depend on the central bank's interest rate. Thus low interest rates on US Treasury bills may give incentives for enhancing the liquidity of less safe assets that exhibit more attractive rates of return. Another example is a capital inflow episode in which liquidity is enhanced by the higher turnover rate of the associated assets.

Financial crises would not be of major concern from a social welfare point of view if it just hit rich bankers. Unfortunately, that is not the case. Often "Main Street" is swept away by "Wall Street" miscalculations. I will argue that liquidity crunch has a direct effect on credit flows and results in ex post overindebtedness because intertemporal transactions strongly depend on the expected liquidity of credit collaterals. Moreover, as a rule, shocks to the credit channel are painful for Main Street because they prompt a search for a new equilibrium output configuration, a time-consuming process.

I highlight in part I the role of liquidity and the many relevant issues that are consistent with views in which liquidity takes center stage. I present in chapter 1 a summary of stylized facts (i.e., empirical essentials) on the recent EM financial crises and the subprime crisis, especially those facts that unroll puzzles for conventional theory. In chapter 2, I summarize the main components of a view centered on liquidity, which I label the liquidity approach. In chapter 3, I outline the established monetary theory and discuss extensions aimed at accounting for relevant liquidity shocks. My central claim is that simple extensions of standard monetary models—which, as a rule, ignore financial complications—help rationalize the implications of liquidity crunch. One lesson is that a liquidity crunch provokes changes in relative prices (e.g., collapse in real estate prices) that cannot be undone by conventional monetary policy, not even quantitative easing. Another lesson is that liquidity crunch and inflation have diametrically opposite effects, depending on whether these phenomena have an impact on consumers or firms—an issue that harks back to the Ohlin–Keynes debate about Keynes's theory of interest (see Davidson 1965; Tsiang 1980).

The extensions above rely on the assumption that liquidity shocks are exogenous, an assumption shared by the new crop of macro models. A distinguishing characteristic of the models in chapter 3 is that results call for minor variations on the conventional representative-individual rational expectations model. This may seem like an oversimplification, but it is in line with the search for "essentials," for these models could be greatly enriched and still core results stemming from liquidity considerations would stay invariant. In fact the chapter illustrates the possibility that richer microfoundations can have misleading policy implications.[4]

In chapters 4 and 5, I discuss slightly more technical models that highlight liquidity issues. I show in chapter 4 that if government debt instruments are endowed with liquidity (an approach originally put forward in a rational-expectations macroeconomic model in Calvo and Végh 1995), some familiar propositions of mainstream monetary theory do not hold, even though all other aspects of the model follow conventional lines. In particular, under sticky prices the central bank would be able to target inflation even though it does not follow Taylor's rule. This result may serve as a warning to central bank technicians that liquidity considerations could substantially change the policy implications of their favorite models. In chapter 5, I show that by fitting standard monetary models with assumptions by which consumers' means of exchange is cash while those of firms are cash and asset-backed securities, one can rationalize the simultaneous occurrences of liquidity crunch and liquidity trap, though the two phenomena, as stated above, look contradictory. I also show that the model offers a straightforward rationale for *secular stagnation* if the liquidity shock is not offset by the creation of other liquid assets.[5]

I present in part II of the book an empirical exploration of the *effects*, and not the causes, of liquidity crunch. I do this in an indirect way by studying *Systemic Sudden Stops* (of capital inflows), under the presumption that the latter are largely triggered by liquidity crunch–type phenomena. I give in chapter 6 an overview of the salient characteristics of Systemic Sudden Stop crises and show that they are different in interesting ways from regular recessions. In particular, I show that in Systemic Sudden Stop, output rebound does not require a recovery of all the pre-crisis sources of credit, even though credit crunch is a central trigger for these episodes. Following Calvo et al. (2006), I call this phenomenon the *phoenix miracle*, in reference to the bird rising from its ashes. I also show that Systemic Sudden Stop crises are associated with less consumption smoothing and more persistent effects than regular recession episodes.

I attempt in chapter 7 to identify the determinants of Sudden Stops (of capital inflows)—a type of credit crunch, very common in EM financial crises—*conditional* on the existence of systemic stringent financial conditions in EMs. The results suggest a strong probability of a Sudden Stop occurring if there is a hike in the EM average risk premium or US interest rates and net international reserves are low.

I Toward the Liquidity Approach

1   Financial Crises and the Slow Mutation of Conventional Wisdom

We have indeed at the moment little cause for pride: as a profession we have made a mess of things.
Hayek (1974)

Worldly wisdom teaches that it is better for reputation to fail conventionally than to succeed unconventionally.
Keynes (1936, ch.12)

This chapter gives a bird's-eye view of major financial crises since 1994 and motivates the conceptual discussion that follows. The focus is not on details but on patterns and puzzles that become apparent when different episodes are discussed, especially those that forced a revision of the conventional paradigm. The first thing that is important is how long it took for the profession to realize that new phenomena were at work, since the tendency for economists was to cling to mainstream models and ignore some key dysfunctional features of the economy, as was once noted by as sharp an observer as John Maynard Keynes. It is fair to say, for instance, that the financial sector's potential dysfunction was largely kept out of the radar until the subprime crisis. Prior to that, the International Monetary Fund's sleuths, for example, were sent out on missions to sniff out almost exclusively for the presence of unsustainable fiscal, current account deficits or overvalued currencies. In the midst of crises they, of course, found problems of that sort, but little attention was paid to vulnerabilities associated with the financial sector—especially those stemming from the rest of the world. The subprime crisis has begun to change this, but as expected after years of neglecting the kinds of financial issues that have besieged developed and emerging market economies (DMs and EMs), the profession is still in the process of groping toward a consensus paradigm.

I will start discussing the onset of, and recovery from, EM crises that took most observers by surprise beginning in the 1990s. These are issues on which I have spent a great deal of time trying to disentangle. Next, I will turn to examine some central features of the 2007 subprime crisis, and end the bird's-eye journey with some remarks about the monetary instruments employed during this episode by DMs, namely central bank interest rates and quantitative easing. The subprime crisis is a much more challenging episode than the equivalent ones in EMs because the former is truly global, it involves global liquidity issues. However, one can detect a link between the two that can be attributed to the workings of liquidity phenomena (for an insightful narrative of the subprime crisis, see Brunnermeier 2009).

Crises in Emerging Market Economies: Onset

The 1990s will go down in history as the beginning of a string of financial crises markedly different from all others since World War II. A salient characteristic of these crises is that they started at a corner of the world but rapidly spread to other areas and economies through channels that, from the perspective of the then prevalent conventional wisdom, generated a great deal of confusion. A striking episode was Mexico's *Tequila* crisis in 1994/5. Mexico was the poster boy of the International Monetary Fund (hereon IMF or just Fund). It had recently signed the North American Free Trade Agreement (NAFTA), and had become a full member of the Organization for Economic Co-operation and Development (OECD)—and yet it suffered a major international credit crunch or Sudden Stop[1] in 1995 that caused its GDP to fall by more than 6 percent, causing major domestic economic and political disruptions. The crisis started in December 1994 and its shock waves hit several markets, including those in Asia and Latin America; tremors were momentarily felt at Wall Street (a fact that was unthinkable prior to the Tequila crisis). Waters calmed down after a while and, besides Argentina, the rest of the world remained virtually unscathed. Thus the first reaction was to see this crisis as a milder replay of the 1980s' Debt Crisis (which also started in Mexico, but involved many other economies). This conjecture was based on the fact that Argentina and Mexico exhibited "large" fiscal and current account deficits.[2] This was a debatable assessment for both economies, but it was a reasonable conjecture, since these were still times when the financial sector, as such, was not in the list of usual suspects. The dominant view was that the financial sector is an effective mechanism for consumption smoothing. Well-run economies would be able to borrow during downturns and lend during bonanzas. The mechanism was not universally available, but that was not attributable to a malfunctioning financial sector. The primary suspect was bad policy making, with fiscal policy heading the list. This conjecture is hard to reject because a rising fiscal deficit usually goes hand in hand with financial crisis. Although the line of causation can go either way, knowing what comes first is very challenging, especially in the short run. For instance, during downturns fiscal revenue tends to decline; thus, unless the government has the power and determination to increase taxes or lower expenditure in the midst of a slump, fiscal deficit will likely rise.

The Tequila crisis was followed by the 1997 Asian crisis and, in rapid succession, the 1998 Russian crisis. The Asian crisis provoked some perplexity in financial circles because these economies had exhibited superb economic performance during a long period of time (the Asian Tigers were in the group) and did not exhibit Latin America–type deficits. The Fund was quick in pointing its commanding finger toward one of its favorite variables, namely the exchange rate. It claimed that the capital sin was pegging the exchange rate without sufficient international reserves to back it up. The financial sector was left completely out of the picture, even though in Korea and Thailand, for example, volatile capital flows took center stage and, in the short run, large currency devaluation failed to stimulate exports for lack of trade credit (see Corsetti et al. 2001). The theory that prevailed at the Fund was unable to establish a causal relationship between devaluation and output collapse. However, despite these conceptual gaps, the conventional wisdom rapidly embraced the view that flexible exchange rates are best unless countries can ensure an ironclad fixed rate vis-à-vis a reserve currency like the US dollar (e.g., Hong Kong). This view was not *de facto* shared by many EMs but, to prevent being labeled unreliable or unserious economies, camouflaged themselves as "floaters" (see Calvo and Reinhart 2002: Levy-Yeyati and Sturzenegger 2005).

Reality gave no respite. The 1998 Russian crisis—the mother of all Sudden Stops before the 2008 Lehman crisis—

hit as a thunderbolt. The best word to characterize the situation in the wake of this episode is "panic." No one seemed to be able to offer a strong rationale for what happened. It hit all EMs with awesome strength, making no distinction between saints and sinners. Asian economies were forced to engage in draconian adjustment: their negative current accounts became sharply positive, while in Latin American economies the average current account (as a share of GDP) went from less than –5 percent to zero on the spur of the moment. And the cause? The proximate cause was Russia's default on *domestic* debt that caught unaware some key hedge funds (e.g., long-term capital management, LTCM). This removed all reasonable excuses for the conventional wisdom to keep ignoring financial sector dysfunctionality, and the expression *new financial architecture* started to grab the headlines.

Figure 1.1 shows the behavior of two key EM variables in the period from January 1991 to January 2004. The shaded region depicts the average EM current account balance, while the solid line corresponds to the average Emerging Market Bond Index spread (EMBI+; henceforth EMBI) published by JPMorgan (where 100 basis points = 1 percent).[3] The period around the Asian crisis is relatively tranquil for EMs, but the Tequila and Russian crises show remarkable phenomena that are worth highlighting. In these two crises, the EMBI shows a very sharp increase within a short span of time. During the Tequila crisis it went from around 500 bps to almost 2000 bps; in the Russian crisis the EMBI rose a tad less but the rise was outstanding nevertheless. What is especially remarkable about these facts is that they did not happen only at the epicenter of the crisis (Mexico in the Tequila or Russia in 1998 crises) but at the whole set of EMs included in the EMBI (see figure 1.1). Thus these crises can

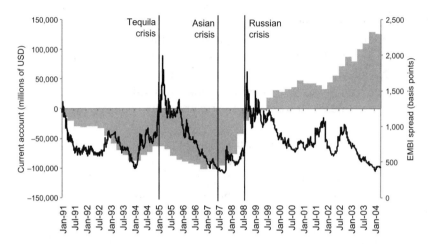

Figure 1.1
External financial conditions for EMs (EMBI sovereign spread and current
account balance in EMs, millions of USD, last four quarters) Included are
Argentina, Brazil, Chile, China, Colombia, Czech Republic, Egypt, Hungary,
India, Indonesia, Israel, Korea, Malaysia, Mexico, Morocco, Pakistan, Peru,
Philippines, Poland, Slovak Republic, South Africa, Thailand, Turkey, and
Venezuela.
Sources: Bloomberg, IFS–International Monetary Fund, national sources

appropriately be labeled *systemic*, and *contagion* (beyond
shocks that can be attributed to standard fundamentals, like
trade flows) becomes a sensible conjecture. Moreover the
EMBI spikes occurred in a very short span of time, suggesting that the market was taken largely by surprise (making
these episodes good candidates to be labeled Sudden Stops).[4]
To be true, some EMs showed large fiscal deficits, but if this
was the main cause behind their instability, one should
expect the EMBI to exhibit a gradual ascent, not the discontinuous type shown in figure 1.1. None of these phenomena
could easily be rationalized by the profession's conventional
wisdom at the time, which contributed in a major way to the

sense helplessness, and hence panic, that prevailed.[5] This suggests, by the way, that the scope of models, the majority of which focus on *individual* countries, should be broadened significantly. Another fact worth highlighting is the sharp reversal of current account deficits after the Asian and Russian crises. This marked an abrupt end of the EM capital inflow episode initiated in the early 1990s, and the beginning of a similar episode in DMs, which can arguably be linked to the subprime crisis in 2007/8.

Something was clearly amiss in the global economy, but the conventional wisdom kept on stressing EM nonfinancial dysfunctionality. This was partly justified by the fact that the epicenters of these crises prior to the subprime were all located at EMs, and the DMs were left virtually unscathed. Thus, even those observers that stressed the relevance of financial issues, tended to conjecture that if EMs had adopted DM market-friendly institutions, crises would have been much milder (see Mishkin 2006). Such an opinion had the weight of history—at least, recent history—on its side, since while EMs underwent these severe financial crises, DMs were coasting along through an exceptionally tranquil period since mid-1980s, labeled "Great Moderation."

Crises in Emerging Market Economies: Recovery

EM crises appear generally to occur after a boom in capital inflows and domestic credit, and widening current account deficits (see Fuentes et al. 2014; Agosin 2012; Mendoza and Terrones 2012). This naturally led to the conjecture that recovery from Sudden Stop, especially if rapid, should entail an infusion of capital inflows and credit. This conjecture was popular in policy circles after the catastrophic fall in output and employment in Argentina following the 2001/2 crisis.

Interestingly, the Argentine government took a strong anti-IMF stance and refused to sign off on a typical Fund's adjustment program. Capital markets shut down tightly, raising expectations that recovery would take years to materialize. However, none of that happened. After a monumentally complicated political transition that saw *five* presidents parade through the *casa rosada* (the downtown presidential palace), output started to grow in 2003 at a record-breaking pace with no help from foreign capital and in the presence of a tiny domestic credit market, as in the proverbial *phoenix miracle*, the bird rising from its ashes. This episode raised the question whether Argentina had found the silver bullet for recovery, or whether this was a run-of-the-mill pattern common to other EM deep financial recessions. The Argentine issue will be discussed in chapter 6 for a group of EM systemic and deep financial crises in the 1980s and early 2000s. It will be clear that Argentina was not a special case. On average, the recovery episodes take place without an equivalent pickup of capital inflows, domestic credit stock/flow, or even investment. Figure 1.2 from Calvo et al. (2006 a) exhibits some of these facts. It shows the sample average for GDP, domestic credit (in real terms), and current account (as a share of output) during the peak-to-recovery period. The unit of time is one year and t denotes the time of the output trough; the dashed lines correspond to domestic credit and current account. The differences between peak and recovery are statistically significant.

These crises are called Systemic Sudden Stops because the rise of the average EMBI and the fall of capital inflows exceed two standard deviations (relative to their historical record; see Izquierdo 2013 for a survey of the literature). Capital inflows include portfolio capital (e.g., bank credit flows) and foreign direct investment. However, the recovery is not fueled by flows in the opposite direction. This is puzzling.

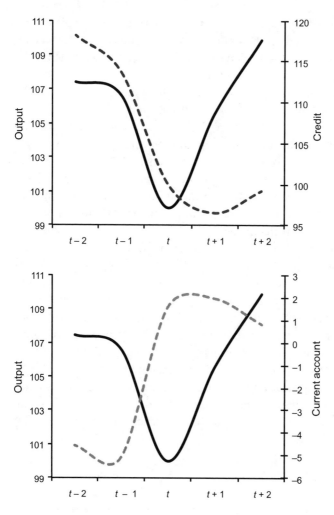

Figure 1.2
Phoenix miracles

Factors that appear to be at the root of the crisis episode are not reversed on the path to recovery. Calvo et al. (2006) conjectures that the explanation may rest on the fact that Sudden Stops entail impairment of some key liquid actual or potential liabilities (e.g., working capital credit lines from the banking sector) that are eventually replaced by alternative credit channels. For example, a stop in bank credit flows may induce firms to engage in interenterprise credit arrangements or to accumulate liquid assets by lowering the rate of investment or increasing retained earnings. This may have been further facilitated by an inflation spike that sharply lowered real wages and by large currency depreciation that increased profits in the tradable sector, and export competitiveness. This evidence suggests that EM crises involve credit or liquidity problems, and that in principle, these problems can be resolved by policies that are aimed at restoring credit or liquidity, issues that were largely ignored in conventional models. The shock is quite different from an earthquake where factors of production are destroyed. Sudden Stops, especially when systemic, destroy liquidity. The solution does not necessarily call for increasing the rate of investment or technical progress, as mainstream macroeconomics leads one to believe. These factors are important for long-run growth but may be much less crucial for recovery after Sudden Stop.[6]

The Subprime Crisis[7]

Problems in the subprime sector were relatively well known but not expected to cause systemic damage. Most subprime mortgages were subject to variable interest rates, and thus it was expected that the rate of nonperforming subprime mortgages would rise as interest rates, which were unusually low, headed back to normal. However, the stock of subprime mortgages was small relative to the total stock of mortgages. and thus hardly anyone expected that problems in the sub-prime market would spread to the other mortgages, and least of all to the global financial market. The dominant view was that if the situation became unstable, lowering the federal funds rate (i.e., the Fed's policy interest rate) by just a few basis points would bring the situation back to normal. This view, plus the fact that US monetary policy was considered excessively lax and likely to fuel inflation, seems to have led the Fed to start raising the federal funds rate in July 2004, and continue doing so until July 2007, when the tremors of the subprime crisis started to be felt. In July 2004 the federal funds rate was 1.03 percent, and it reached its peak at 5.26 percent in July 2007 (see figure 1.3). Afterward, as the sever-ity of the crisis became apparent, but before the Lehman crisis, the Fed rapidly pushed the rate slightly below 2

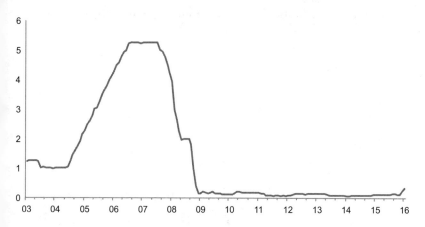

Figure 1.3
US federal funds rate
Source: Federal Reserve Bank of St. Louis

percent, and pushed it down to virtually zero as the Lehman crisis erupted. This unusual federal funds rate's pattern is a clear indication that the Fed was overwhelmed by the turn of events.

Contrary to expectations, the repercussions of the sub-prime mortgage market crisis on the global capital market did not take long to be felt. A dramatic illustration is provided by the TED spread, a measure of banking risk (see figure 1.4).[8] Its high point was unprecedented, given that during tranquil periods the TED spread crawls along very close to zero. In response, monetary policy in the US, EU and UK became boldly anticyclical, resulting in a pronounced decline in the TED spread. This shows the impressive power that DM central banks wielded for quickly stabilizing the situation in the financial sector, and suggests that liquidity played a central role in these events. It is worth noting, incidentally, that in the Russian 1998 crisis, EMs did not get equivalent support from hard-currency central banks. As a result the EMBI took more than four years after the onset of

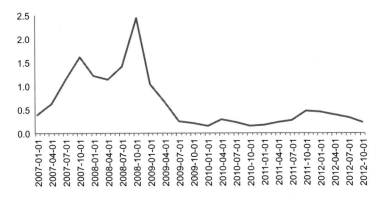

Figure 1.4
TED spread (%)
Source: Federal Reserve Bank of St. Louis

the Russian crisis to return to the level that prevailed prior to crisis (see figure 1.1). So, once again, we see the importance of liquidity factors.

While expansive monetary policy was highly effective for lowering risk perception in the financial sector, another big surprise was lying in wait: the real sector in both DMs and EMs suffered major slumps. US output, for instance, fell by more than 4 percent from peak to trough, and took about five years to recover its pre-crisis level (twice the recovery time for EMs, recall figure 1.2). The financial slump was another big surprise because, according to the conventional wisdom, the Great Depression in the 1930s would not have occurred if monetary policy had prevented CPI or PPI deflation. The lesson was heeded by central banks during the subprime crisis but the reflationary policy was not enough to prevent a deep and long-lasting output slump. In addition jobless recovery—a common feature in US recessions—was exacerbated (see chapter 6 and Calvo et al. 2012). Many observers attribute this phenomenon to the massive destruction of credit instruments (or, as I argue in this book, liquid assets and/or means of exchange) that paralyzed the wheels of credit and commerce, both domestic and international trade.

The impact of the subprime crisis on EMs is also interesting. Figure 1.5, clearly shows that the EMs appeared to be shielded at the inception of the crisis. To be true, the EMBI started to rise from 2007-IV, but this was the result of the collapse in US interest rates (recall figure 1.3). A more relevant measure of EM financial conditions is given by the yield, which as shown in figure 1.5 stayed flat until the Lehman episode. These facts led observers to conjecture that EMs had "decoupled" from DMs. But decoupling did not last long. The Lehman crisis brought decoupling to an abrupt end: the EMBI's instant rise exceeded 400 basis points.

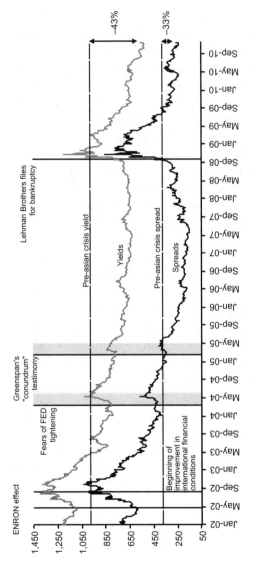

Figure 1.5
Emerging markets and subprime crisis
Source: Bloomberg

Interestingly, though, financial conditions improved very rapidly hand in hand with the TED spread, confirming the effectiveness of DM expansive monetary policy for stabilizing the financial sector and, furthermore, reinforcing the view that *financial* disarray was at the heart of the crisis.

The Lehman crisis' impact on the real sector was global but contrary to expectations, the EMs were able to recover much faster than DMs (see figure 1.6). Figure 1.7 shows that capital flows toward EMs displayed a clear upward trend, with Foreign Direct Investment (FDI) taking the lion's share.[9]

Consequently it would be fair to say that after 2009 EMs have again shown clear signs of decoupling. The question

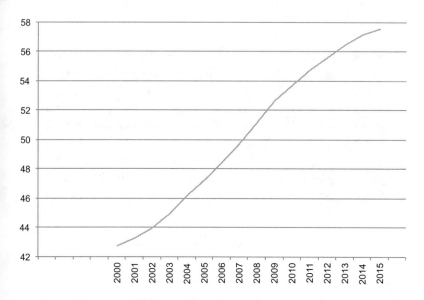

Figure 1.6
Emerging market and developed economies (% of world GDP)
Source: WEO, October 2015, based on purchasing power parity

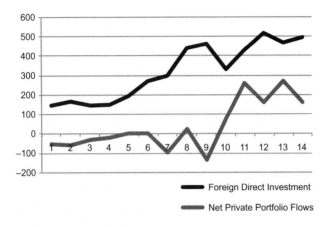

Figure 1.7
Capital inflows in emerging and developed economies (billion USD)
Source: WEO October 2015

remains, however, whether this regained vitality is sustain-
able. Doubts remain. Markets have become very sensitive to
financial news. For example, rumors about Fed tightening in
August 2013 sent strong shock waves to EMs (an episode
popularly known as "Taper Tantrum"), and earlier champi-
ons became Fragile Markets on the spur of the moment (see
Sahay et al. 2014). This, again, suggests that factors other
than standard fundamentals are at work. Liquidity and its
fragility, an issue that will be explored in chapter 2, are my
primary suspects.

Quantitative Easing, Tapering, and Central Bank Interest Rates

After the Lehman crisis, DM central banks pushed their
interest rates to the ground, but, as discussed above, they
failed to have the expected salutary effect on output. At that

point, the Fed took the lead by adopting a type of unconventional monetary policy that goes by the name of "quantitative easing" (QE).[10] This policy can take different forms. One important form consists of central banks purchasing private or public assets in exchange for money (more precisely, *base money*, i.e., the sum of currency in circulation and deposits of banks and other depository institution at the central bank). For example, the Fed was involved in a massive program of purchasing mortgage-backed securities (MBS) from government-sponsored enterprises, like Fannie Mae and Freddie Mac, at book value. These are usually called "toxic" assets. At first, interest rates and QE appeared to be alternative ways of pumping in liquidity into the financial system. However, interest rate policy proved to be more *neutral* than QE, since the latter can be used to extend credit to specific private sub-sectors while the former relies on financial intermediaries to do the job.[11] The purchase of MBS is a good example of nonneutrality; it was motivated by trying to stimulate credit flows toward the real estate sector, the epicenter of the subprime crisis. But there are other forms that QE can take. One such form is "operation twist," which consists of purchasing long-term for short-term public debt obligations by selling short-term Treasury bills held by the Fed. Short-term debt does not change the size of the Fed's balance sheet, because it just entails a change in the *composition* of the central bank's asset side of its balance sheet. Recent research (see Krishnamurthy and Vissing-Jorgensen 2013) claims that the purchase of toxic assets had a larger impact on the US economy than operation twist. This makes intuitive sense, since when interest rates are low, operation twist is akin to purchasing one 20-dollar bill with two 10-dollar bills; in contrast, purchasing toxic assets entails purchasing illiquid and devalued assets at book value with fresh-minted dollar bills, the ultimate form of global liquidity.

There is a debate about the effect of DM QE on EMs. Some analysts believe that QE sends a wall of liquidity to EMs, which account for the larger capital flows toward EMs after the Lehman episode (see Turner 2013). In my view, a much bigger impact was caused by low interest rates on highly liquid DM public debt obligations, such as US Treasury bills and bonds. This topic will be more fully discussed in chapter 6, but the central argument is quite obvious. It dwells on two pillars. One pillar has been mentioned above and can be summarized as follows: QE has been hardly effective in changing the stock of liquidity, or, if it did, it helped open the credit market *in DMs* (as is the case of toxic-asset purchases). The second pillar is that a central impact of the subprime in DMs has been a massive destruction of "safe assets" (see Caballero et al. 2008; Caballero and Farhi 2015; Gorton and Metrick 2012; Calvo 2012 a). These are essential instruments in modern capitalist economies. A destruction of safe means of exchange could grind trading to a halt, giving incentives to the financial sector to develop new safe assets or enhance old liquid assets to make them safer. Here is where interest rates on super-safe assets like US Treasury bills can make a difference. Low interest on super-safe assets gives rise to a search for yield on actual or potential safe assets, increasing the incentives to generate assets akin to safe assets. Therefore it is to be expected that the private financial sector will increase the supply of safer assets. Possible candidates are EM assets because those economies were relatively free from the financial disarray in which shadow banks were involved. The problem is that the associated flows are, first and foremost, in search of liquidity, making the demand for EM liquid assets highly sensitive to DM safe-assets interest rates.

This view implies that it would be a mistake to extrapolate the relatively benign impact of QE tapering and to discount the effects of a rise in the US federal funds rate. The experiments are very different. In fact Calvo et al. (1993) alerted that the capital-inflow episode in Latin America in the early 1990s could end up in a financial crisis the moment the Fed started to jack up interest rates from the then historically depressed levels (3 percent, a level that would be considered high for present standards!). Unfortunately, this turned out not to be an empty warning: the Tequila crisis coincided with a rise in the federal funds rate to about 6 percent. Calvo et al. (1993) employed US *short-term* interest rates as one of the explanatory variables, which was criticized because, if one ignores liquidity considerations, it can reasonably be argued that EM capital flows respond to changes in *long-term* interest rates. However, if liquidity is a major consideration, as argued above, DM short-term interest rates will have a large effect on those flows, which illustrates the relevance of accounting for liquidity factors. This issue will be pursued in the next chapter.

Summary and Next Step

• Major financial crises since the 1990s started at a corner of the world economy and spread across the world like wildfire.
• Asset prices and output plummeted in the face of stable standard "fundamentals." True, "fundamentals" deteriorated during crises, but this was largely an *outcome*, not a cause.
• These features are shared by emerging and developed market economies alike. Market reforms are probably necessary to avoid further crises, but there is still no role model that can be followed as policy guide.

• The challenge is to develop a framework in which financial crises have causes that go far beyond standard "fundamentals" and have deleterious effects on regions and markets that, at first, may appear largely disconnected to the epicenter (or initial location) of the crisis.

• For someone raised in general equilibrium theory, these features suggest "equilibrium multiplicity" and the existence of coordinating factors that suddenly causes the economy to switch equilibriums. Alternatively, these features suggest the existence of pecuniary externalities coupled with significant nonlinearities. Both of these insights are being explored in the current literature.

• In this book I take a step back and look for "essentials" that could be claimed to be common to most crises. I will attempt to persuade the reader that "liquidity," a concept that has been downplayed in mainstream macro models, offers a plausible clue for the financial instability of capitalist economies, especially those that are directly or indirectly tied to sophisticated financial systems.

• At the risk of oversimplification, in the rest of this part of the book I will explore the insights that arise from frameworks in which liquidity takes center stage (which characterize what I call the liquidity approach). In particular, I will explore the impact of liquidity crunch episodes on the *real* economy.

• The discussion and models in part I should be seen as complementary to the current crisis literature, especially models in which issues of liquidity and collateral are given pride of place.

2   The Liquidity Approach to Financial Crises[1]

... the use of money is enough in itself to make a free market system potentially unstable; and that the higher the degree of development, or sophistication, that it exhibits the greater does the danger of instability become .... It is a "psychological" instability, not a mechanical, which is in question: so it cannot be remedied by the application of a formula, as so many, both then and in later days, have been tempted to suppose.

Hicks (1982, p. 9)

As I noted in the previous chapter, "liquidity" or "means of exchange" problems are factors that cannot be ignored in a reasonable narrative of financial crises. In this chapter I take a more *theoretical* tack and explore the potential explanatory power of the view that puts liquidity at the center of these crisis episodes, a view that I will call the Liquidity Approach (to financial crisis). The Liquidity Approach focuses on the primary triggers and possible magnifiers of financial crises. I argue that the Liquidity Approach can offer a rationale for central and puzzling phenomena that cannot be easily explained by mainstream macro models. An example to which I devote some attention is the striking resilience of the output price of fiat or paper money ("cash" or "currency," for short) in developed market economies. DMs were at the epicenter of the subprime crisis. Nevertheless, the demand for DM cash (particularly the US dollar and dollar-denominated assets fully guaranteed by the US government, e.g., Treasury bills; "dollar" for short) has exhibited a sizable increase (Liquidity Trap). This puzzle is exacerbated by the simultaneous occurrence of a large price meltdown in other DM liquid assets (liquidity crunch).

I start with a definition of liquidity and its sharp demise (liquidity crunch), and continue with a discussion of the strength of DM currencies during crisis, a fact that stands in sharp contrast with the weakness of emerging market currencies under similar circumstances (see chapter 6). The centerpiece of this section will be the Price Theory of Money proposed by Keynes (1936). I argue that liquidity crunch can give rise to credit Sudden Stop, and a *coordinated* fall in aggregate demand with dire consequences for output and employment. Making these points does not require abandoning the assumption of rational expectations, or assuming animal spirits that *coordinate* gloomy views about the marginal efficiency of investment by CEOs, or trigger massive thriftiness attacks on the part of consumers.

A lesson of the chapter is that discussion of liquidity issues reveals aspects of modern economies that are radically different from the conventional view and show the relevance of central banks and financial regulators for preventing and managing financial crises.[2] However, the discussion will also make it evident that *liquidity* opens up a variety of questions for which we do not have clear answers.

Liquidity and Its Demise: Liquidity Crunch

"Liquidity" is a slippery concept, and is all the more so given the lack of attention it has received from economists since

World War II. In the conventional model, liquidity is represented by something called "money," and a central proposition is that "money is a veil." This view, taken to an extreme, is tantamount to saying that money is essential for the determination of the price level, and nothing else. Under this lens, monetary policy has no significant effect on output or employment (i.e., money is "neutral," in the macroeconomist's lingo).[3] Of course, standard Keynesian models give a nonneutral role to money, but this is achieved by assuming some sort of nominal price/wage rigidity, not by delving deeply into the nature of money or liquidity. Thus, aside from the distinction between outside and inside money to incorporate in the analysis commercial banks as producers of inside money (e.g., sight deposits), conventional macroeconomics has had little to contribute to the liquidity discussion.

The subprime crisis and the type of phenomena highlighted in the previous chapter have given a strong impetus to the liquidity literature. A dominant view that emerges from that literature is that liquidity is an essential characteristic of means of exchange, and that its effectiveness in that role is an increasing function of the ability of making means of exchange equivalent to a basket of highly tradable goods (i.e., items that *directly* enter utility or production functions), at highly predictable relative prices and involving relatively low search costs. Models differ as to the specifics, but a term that is becoming increasingly popular is "pledgeability." The word is especially central in models that highlight the credit market (e.g., Kiyotaki and Moore 1997; Holmström and Tirole 1998, 2011). Pledgeable is the share of a good/asset that can be easily transformed into a basket of highly tradable goods.[4] In models with a few goods (which hide the imprecision of the expression "basket of goods"), pledgeability offers respectable foundations for the liquidity concept. By "respectable," I mean foundations that facilitate inserting the model into the general equilibrium Arrow–Debreu model—expanded to account for asymmetric information or agency considerations—without having to model objects like "money" that have always looked alien or redundant in that kind of framework.

However, the appeal of those models to the professional economist is obtained at a cost, since it ignores assets that are deemed highly liquid in practice but have no intrinsic value and no predefined claim on goods. A classic example is fiat or paper money. To discuss this issue, it is useful to extend the discussion and define two types of pledgeabilities, namely *intrinsic* and *extrinsic*. Intrinsic pledgeability is the concept mentioned above—the ability of transforming a given good or asset into a basket of highly tradable goods. On the other hand, extrinsic pledgeability is the ability to quickly get real goods on the *expectation* that someone else will accept the liquid asset in question in exchange for a basket of goods. In other words, an intrinsically liquid asset contains real goods in its core, while extrinsically liquid assets have none. To transform the latter into goods, there is at least one more step that has to be taken, involving at least another agent that is willing to accept the extrinsically liquid asset for real goods. As indicated, fiat money belongs to that group.

From the point of view of an individual, the difference between intrinsic or extrinsic liquidity is not major. However, in models where utility and production functions are the essential ingredients of human welfare, extrinsic liquidity appears as a flimsier form of liquidity than intrinsic liquidity. Extrinsic liquidity is a concept alien to Robinson Crusoe, for example. Extrinsic liquidity is liable to vanish by the simple fact that individuals suddenly refuse to surrender goods in exchange. This type of shock can take place even though there is no major shock to utility or production functions—no earthquake that destroys real assets, for instance. For the man in the street (including many economists in the immediate aftermath of the shock), the shock would look as mysterious as a thunderbolt for the primitive man. These shocks characterize most liquidity crunch episodes in recent financial crises (see chapter 1). The following discussion will focus on the economics of extrinsic liquidity and liquidity crunch episodes.

A liquidity crunch can be triggered by factors that are not mere illusions or delusions. Consider the familiar example in which there is only one commercial bank.[5] The bank is funded by demand deposits denominated in terms of cash, purchases illiquid assets (i.e., makes loans that are hard to exchange for cash on call), and holds a precautionary stock of money to cover deposit withdrawals. Under normal circumstances, bank deposits are close substitutes of cash, which leads banks to feel safe lending a large share of deposits and holding a small amount of cash in their coffers for unusual deposit withdrawals. This situation I call "the good equilibrium"; it characterizes capitalist economies in "tranquil,' non-crisis times. However, one cannot discount the existence of a "bad equilibrium" in which depositors expect that a large number of fellow depositors will try to take their cash out of the bank. In that situation, depositors have incentives to do the same because they know that the bank coffers are pretty slim. If every depositor attempts to get her money out of the bank at the same time, the bank cannot honor the contract to exchange deposits for cash on call—and goes bankrupt. Bank runs impair the liquidity of bank deposits suddenly, causing liquidity crunch.

Bank runs were the main motivation for the establishment of central banks, which, as the subprime crisis has demonstrated, help stave off harmful bank runs. But, especially in DMs, only a small share of the stock of extrinsically liquid assets is protected by a central bank. Thus it would be fair to say that *liquidity crunch is an endemic disease in economies where extrinsically liquid assets play an important role*. The associated crisis, it should be noted, is not incompatible with *rational expectations* and therefore could be rationalized in terms of mainstream theory (see chapter 3).

A Resilient Dollar—The Price Theory of Money to the Rescue!

The subprime crisis has shown that *not all extrinsically liquid assets are equally fragile*. The dollar, for example, has exhibited remarkable resilience during the subprime crisis. This is very puzzling because dollar bills have no intrinsic value and the Fed makes no commitment to exchange dollar bills for goods and services.[6] In fact the dollar's "fundamentals" are weaker than bank deposits because the latter are collateralized with claims on real private sector assets, whereas dollar bills have no collateral.[7] So, why was the dollar so resilient during the subprime crisis?

To answer this question, it is convenient, first, to discuss the reasons why the relative price of cash in terms of goods and services is positive.[8] The microeconomic literature has explored different reasons for this to be the case, such as legal tender or the obligation to settle tax liabilities with cash. However, as argued by Calvo (2012 a), these explanations are not persuasive, especially in a multi-currency world. An explanation that has been largely ignored by the profession and that I find very appealing—although admittedly incomplete—was proposed in Keynes's *General Theory*. He writes: "the fact that contracts are fixed, and wages are usually somewhat stable in terms of money, *unquestionably* plays a large part in attracting to money so high a liquidity-premium" (1936, chapter 17; italics are mine). By "liquidity premium" Keynes means the difference between the market's output value of money and its intrinsic value (virtually zero).

I discuss Keynes's conjecture in Calvo (2012 a) and call it the Price Theory of Money (PTM). Intuitively, the PTM asserts that *money's output value cannot be nil in equilibrium because economic agents set several key nominal prices/wages in advance, thereby offering a ground-up output guarantee to cash.*[9] It is extraordinary that to this day this kind of guarantee that holds in all capitalist economies has largely been overlooked by the micro- and macro-literature. I suspect the omission stems from the lack of a deep discussion of liquidity issues in macroeconomics and also the obliteration of price/wage stickiness issues from microeconomics.

The PTM offers a partial rationale for the resilience of the dollar relative to other liquid assets. Most prices and wages ("prices," for short) in the United States, for instance, are set in dollars and show some degree of temporary stickiness, validating the assumptions of the PTM. This puts the dollar in a privileged position relative to other extrinsically liquid assets, like asset-backed securities (ABS). There is no commitment—comparable to that enjoyed by cash—to exchange ABS for goods and services on short notice. This does not imply that ABS and other financial assets have no real backstop. Market makers do that to some extent. But the stickiness of market makers' prices is short-lived compared to labor contracts, and during financial crises there are several instances in which market makers have shut down, paralyzing security market transactions and creating a situation in which market prices disappeared into "thin air" (see Mehrling 2011; Financial Times 2014). This situation debilitates the real anchor enjoyed by liquid assets other than cash. It helps rationalize a scenario in which, say, ABS prices collapse while the demand for cash rises and liquidity trap takes place (for a formal model displaying this feature, see chapter 5).

Finally, the output guarantee for cash becomes even stronger/more credible if prices are set in an uncoordinated fashion, and there is no significant bunching of price revisions, a realistic situation that the literature calls *staggered prices*. To see this, notice that if, contrariwise, all prices were set at the same time, price setters could all simultaneously change the unit of account in which their prices are quoted—from dollars to bitcoin, for example—keeping intact relative prices. The latter does not hold under staggered pricing, which generates disincentives for marginal price setters to pull out of the pack and set their prices in a different unit of account.

The PTM implies that even fiat money involves some output pledgeability. However, fiat money's liquidity is fundamentally *extrinsic*, since in most cases there is no formal or legal commitment to exchange fiat money for goods. Its acceptability as a means of exchange may be enhanced by the existence of staggered prices but, as a rule, fiat currencies are just worthless pieces of paper/metal (relative to what they can command in the market)—a far cry from, say, a gold watch used as collateral in a pawnshop whose market value normally exceeds, by a wide margin, that of the corresponding collateralized credit. The lack of predetermined output pledge may detract from fiat money's liquidity. However, there is an important offsetting factor. An advantage of fiat money over other assets with pledgeable goods is that, unless the pledge is expressed in terms of money—which would bring us back to the PTM—those pledges are specified in terms of a narrow set of goods (a house, a gold watch, a laptop, etc.), while fiat money offers command on all goods whose prices are predetermined in terms of the corresponding unit of account. This gives an additional reason why a liquidity trap can occur during a liquidity crunch episode. Moreover it helps explain why a *reserve currency* like the dollar, a global unit of account, can be subject to a liquidity trap while EM currencies undergo liquidity crunch or are victims of capital flight. This will be discussed next.

Multiple Currencies

The resilience of the dollar during the subprime crisis, abstracted from the fact that there are many different fiat monies in circulation. The latter opens up the possibility that the degree of output anchoring differs across currencies. Actually the US dollar holds a prominent position because the US economy is very large, US domestic prices are set in dollars, and even import prices are remarkably insensitive to swings in the dollar exchange rates (see Dornbusch 1987; Gopinath et al. 2010). Moreover *the dollar is a worldwide unit of account*. Commodity prices are set in dollars, and until the Lehman crisis, oil prices were somewhat sticky in dollar terms, thanks to OPEC's quantitative controls on oil supply. In fact the dollar has been a key unit of account in global financial transactions for an extended period of time, and dollar-denominated financial markets dominate those of other major currencies. To wit, the eurodollar market has no parallel in a US–euro or US–sterling market. Nevertheless, the dollar preeminence is not guaranteed going forward because there are elements of self-fulfilling prophesy behind the resilience of the US dollar. This is important to keep in mind in assessing stimulus packages based on making dollar holding less attractive, such as through higher dollar inflation or negative nominal rate of interest on money holdings (e.g., Gesell's Stamped Money proposal; see Keynes 1936, ch. 23).

Emerging market fiat monies represent an interesting contrast. In many EMs, for instance, the dollar or euro are units of account for domestic transactions, especially for big-ticket items like real estate and luxury cars. Moreover the pass-through to domestic prices from changes in the exchange rate is large relative to DMs for EMs with a history of high inflation (Choudhri and Hakura 2001; Burstein and Gopinath 2014). Thus the real anchor of EM fiat monies—their PTM component, if you will—is likely to be significantly weaker than that of the dollar. EM policy makers are keenly aware of this and are adamant to let their currencies fluctuate—a phenomenon studied in Calvo and Reinhart (2000, 2002), and labeled "fear of floating." Under the PTM perspective, fear of floating is equivalent to hardening the real anchor of EM cash by pegging to fiat monies that are perceived as being firmly anchored onto the real sector (which I call "safe monies"), like the dollar. This is not cost free because it induces EMs to accumulate costly international reserves, namely a stock of safe monies and liquid assets backed up by their corresponding central banks. Thus fear of floating shows that EMs have implicitly embraced a system akin to that of Bretton Woods, in which pegged but adjustable parities are the rule. Many EMs accomplish this unilaterally, without relying on international financial institutions (IFIs).[10] Consequently, the stock of international reserves in the hands of EMs has skyrocketed (e.g., see Obstfeld et al. 2010), and this, in a way, has further reinforced the real anchor of DM currencies—particularly the dollar, given that it still has the lion's share in EM international reserves.[11]

Liquidity Crunch and Sudden Stops: Collateral Damage

A liquidity crunch episode, like the one that took place around the Lehman crisis, can have severe effects on credit flows. Large and largely unexpected contractions of credit flows are called Sudden Stops (SS). SS have been shown to cause major disruptions in the real sector.[12] SS can hit an economy as a whole, as was the case in EM financial crises, or just a subsector, as in the US real estate market in the wake of the Lehman crisis episode (in which case term-mismatch between assets and liabilities may wreak chaos, even if contracts are denominated in the same unit of account; see below).

Well-anchored fiat monies can oil the wheels of the credit market. The credit market deals with intertemporal transactions in which, say, *today* one agent supplies a piece of bread to another in exchange for a promise from the buyer to deliver a (usually larger) piece of bread *tomorrow*. A simple way to carry out this transaction is for the buyer to issue an IOU. However, assessing the credibility of the IOU calls for substantial information on the part of the seller. A way around this problem is for the buyer to pay with money that is well anchored in terms of output. Other liquid assets are also regularly utilized for intertemporal transactions. But, if PTM considerations or a lender of last resort do not protect the output value of those assets, they could be subject to liquidity crunch. It follows that a liquidity crunch episode can have severe effects on credit flows. Moreover, as discussed above, during an SS/liquidity crunch episode not all liquid assets are hit alike, and may have disparate impact on collateral values.

This is a critical issue that deserves greater attention. Consider the case of mortgage-backed securities (MBS) that played an important role in facilitating housing market credit, but suffered a major liquidity setback during the Lehman crisis. Arguably, the shock increased intermediation costs in the real estate market, which reduced the demand for housing and provoked a meltdown in real estate prices. Developed market central banks reacted by increasing the supply of *base money* (i.e., cash in the hands of the public and banks), a different type of liquid asset than MBS. This had a positive effect on the CPI (the consumer price index) but did not prevent a massive fall in house prices. Thus, even though cash and MBS are two forms of liquid assets, central banks were unable to offset the effects of liquidity crunch on MBS. Chapter 3 will discuss this in terms of a formal model.

The point above is worth stressing because the conventional wisdom prior to the subprime crisis took to heart Friedman and Schwartz's (1963) conjecture that the 1930s Great Depression would have being a regular recession had the Fed increased money supply and stopped producer and consumer prices from falling precipitously. Fisher (1933), in particular, discussed a mechanism that helps explain why the massive price deflation that took place in that episode caused major financial disruption. He argued that price deflation could give rise to *unplanned overindebtedness*, given that most debts were denominated in dollar terms and were non-state contingent (a phenomenon that he labeled "debt deflation"). I do not disagree with the basic intuition. However, the previous paragraph suggests that monetary expansion might not have been powerful enough to prevent the fall of real estate *relative prices* during the subprime crisis, *even if debt deflation* were prevented.[13] Furthermore, since US mortgage contracts are set in nominal terms, preventing a large capital loss for mortgage debtors would have called for consumer or producer prices to *increase* by around 30 percent on impact! Implementing this was very difficult in view of the liquidity trap phenomenon. Besides, if successful, this policy would have been equivalent to a major devaluation of the dollar's real anchor which, as pointed out above, could have debilitated the safety of the dollar unit of account—the corner stone of the global financial system—possibly exacerbating recession and causing severe political backlash.

Interestingly, a phenomenon akin to debt deflation occurred in EM financial crises, even though these economies were free from liquidity trap (if anything, they suffered from capital flight) and, on average, they exhibited sharp inflation spikes (see chapter 6). Debt deflation–like phenomena happened because a large share of EM debt (not exclusively external) was denominated in terms of foreign exchange—another consequence of emerging markets' perceived weak real anchors (see Eichengreen et al. 2005). Thus large devaluation resulted in a sizable increase in external debt as a share of GDP. To avoid debt deflation under these circumstances would therefore call for tightening monetary policy to prevent large currency devaluation, exacerbating the slump!

Even if overindebtedness is avoided by resorting to aggressive monetary/fiscal policy—inclusive of debt forgiveness and rescheduling—liquidity crunch could still have a deleterious effect on the credit channel. For example, it may be hard for house credit to bounce back to the situation prior to crisis, unless the market for MBS is thoroughly repaired, which is not automatically granted by protecting house debtors. Absent full repair of extrinsically liquid assets, a liquidity crunch may generate a saving's glut, given that the increase in savers' expenditure is unlikely to be offset by the *forced* decrease in dissavers' expenditure (due to the liquidity shock). Saving's glut is more likely to arise if the episode takes most agents by surprise, giving little time for saving flows to find alternative outlets. Moreover a Keynesian impasse, where output is the adjustment variable, cannot be discounted if the central bank succeeds in staving off price deflation.[14] However, recession would be less acute for economies that can generate a surge in exports. This mechanism operated in EMs (thanks to weak currencies!) and was instrumental for quick recovery (see chapter 6). But it is worth noting that EM export expansion took place during the Great Moderation period in DMs (the destination of a large share of EM exports) and that output recovery was nevertheless far from instantaneous. Moreover there is some evidence pointing out to a negative impact of financial crisis on output trend (see Cerra and Saxena 2008).[15] This suggests that even in cases in which demand expansion can be quickly triggered from abroad, liquidity considerations could have long-lasting detrimental effects. (These issues are further discussed in chapter 6.)

Liquidity crunch of financial assets can also have an impact on the relative price of factors of production. As noted above, access to credit is facilitated, and attendant interest rates lowered, by being able to post liquid collateral assets. However, at least two types of collaterals can be distinguished: intrinsic and extrinsic. [16] Intrinsic collateral is the collateral inherent in the goods that are purchased on credit. For example, a laptop that can be repossessed in case of default exhibits an intrinsic collateral linked to its price in the secondary market. However, financing the costs associated with a search for new employees has hardly any intrinsic collateral. Arguably, projects that are more extrinsic-collateral intensive are likely to be hit harder by liquidity crunch on financial assets. This conjecture is explored in Calvo et al. (2012) and in chapter 6 under the assumption that capital accumulation projects are less extrinsic-collateral intensive than projects related to the labor market. An implication is that liquidity crunch hits the labor market by either increasing the rate of unemployment or depressing real wages relative to pre-crisis levels, even if output recovers its pre-crisis level.

Collateral distortions can also impinge on growth. Reis (2013), for instance, argues that Portugal's dismal growth since the beginning of the twenty-first century can be partly explained by the existence of collateral constraints and other financial frictions that apparently helped channel the increase in external credit associated with the adoption of the euro to relatively unproductive sectors. His model is very interesting because it can rationalize a case in which the negative growth effects of capital inflows are so strong that, contrary to most capital inflow episodes in EMs, even a large surge of capital inflows fails to give rise to consumption boom.

Policy Challenges under Liquidity Deflation, and Other Forms of Liquidity Mischief

A natural implication of the PTM is that there may be cases in which an increase in money supply may fail to generate higher liquidity, limiting the effectiveness of monetary policy during periods of liquidity shortage. Below I discuss this topic under the title "liquidity deflation," and argue that it offers a novel explanation for liquidity trap. The section continues with a discussion of shadow banking, and the effects of low international interest rates. These topics have "liquidity" as a common thread and are linked to dismal outcomes.

Hence, paraphrasing Friedman (1992), this chapter's examples can be viewed as different manifestations of *liquidity mischief*.

Liquidity Deflation.   Liquidity depends on market characteristics. The PTM, for instance, stresses the role of sticky prices cum demand-determined output as a factor behind the liquidity of fiat money and helps explain why there are cases in which fiat money's output price does not suffer a major collapse. However, the output backup is limited; it depends not only on sticky prices but also on suppliers' readiness to expand output as demand goes up. Suppose, for the sake of the argument, that money's output backup has an upper bound, Q. Therefore, if real monetary balances exceed Q, the excess has no output backup and would be subject to liquidity crunch. This is an important observation because it shows that under liquidity crunch conditions, price level deflation may not help increase *real* liquidity, even though it increases the stock of real monetary balances. Thus, under severe liquidity shortage conditions, Pigou's real-balance effect may stop working, even though nominal prices are perfectly downward flexible. Likewise Pigou's effect may not work if money supply increases when real monetary balances have reached Q, even though nominal prices are upward inflexible. In both examples money's liquidity per unit of money supply *falls* if real monetary balances are pushed beyond Q. Mainstream models in which money's liquidity is taken for granted and is invariant to its real value miss this feature. I will call this effect *liquidity deflation* (LD) because the concept is a close relative of debt deflation (see Fischer 1933, and discussion below).

LD is a relatively novel concept, and I am afraid it runs the risk of being misunderstood. A banking example may help intuition. Consider the T-account for a banking system with deposits on the liability side (which I will identify with *money*) and land on the asset side. The nominal value of land is assumed to be proportional to the price level. Under these conditions a fall in the price level increases real monetary balances (i.e., the real value of bank deposits), but it provokes a capital loss for the banking system because land prices fall. Thus the increase in real monetary balances does not necessarily translate into higher liquidity, since the fall in the price level may increase the chances of a bank run, making deposits less safe. Notice, incidentally, that LD in this example could be modeled as a pecuniary externality for individual banks and households because, in an atomistic highly competitive environment, LD would be invariant to changes in the demand for money of individual agents. In the example, LD is only triggered by changes in the *aggregate* stock of real monetary balances.

The relevance of LD can be illustrated by reference to the equilibrium condition in the money market (i.e., the LM curve). Consider the following equilibrium equation:

$$\frac{M}{P} + Z(m^e) = L(i, Y),$$

where M, P, i, and Y stand for money, the price level, nominal interest rate, and output, respectively. Moreover m^e stands for real money balance, M/P at equilibrium. Function L is the demand for *liquidity*, and Z stands for the new money liquidity component. Except for Z, the equation above is a standard money market equilibrium condition in textbook models.

Given that, at equilibrium, $m^e = M/P$, across equilibrium points the equation above can be expressed as follows:

$$\frac{M}{P} + Z\left(\frac{M}{P}\right) = L(i, Y)$$

To capture the LD effect, I assume that the new money liquidity component declines with the stock of *equilibrium* real monetary balance. Formally, I assume $Z' < 0$. Hence the left-hand side of this equation has an ambiguous sign with respect to real monetary balances. The case stressed in the verbal discussion above corresponds to a situation in which the positive and negative effects with respect to M/P offset each other. This is an interesting special case because it would be observationally equivalent to liquidity trap as usually depicted in textbook models. In textbook models, liquidity trap corresponds to a situation in which the demand for money becomes infinitely elastic with respect to the interest rate i. If the left-hand side of the equation is invariant with respect to M/P, pumping in more money does not change the *supply* of liquidity, and therefore equilibrium will hold with constant i.

The LD phenomenon is not only applicable to money. It also applies to all types of bonds denominated in terms of cash that are not fully indexed to the price level. The rise in the price of US Treasury bills, for example, may find increasing difficulty in generating greater overall liquidity because, as suggested by LD, their market value depends more heavily on extrinsic liquidity considerations than on standard 'fundamentals', including the factors associated with the PTM. This is important because it shows that liquidity shortage cannot necessarily be alleviated by a fall in the price level or the rise in the price of ultra-safe assets (i.e., assets whose payoff is fully guaranteed in terms of cash). This observation sheds further light on the current literature on safe asset shortage, and casts some doubts on the effectiveness of trying to relieve such shortage by expanding the supply of public debt in reserve-currency economies (e.g., see Caballero and Farhi 2015). In fact LD helps rationalize the point of view that is becoming increasingly popular these days—given the tepid recovery of the global economy after the subprime crisis—that QE is perilously losing its "punch."

Interestingly, while QE may lose its punch, the central bank interest rate may still keep its own. I will denote the central bank interest rate by i^m, which, in the present context, I will identify as the interest rate on money.[17] Hence the opportunity cost of holding money boils down to $i - i^m$, and the equation above becomes

$$\frac{M}{P} + Z\left(\frac{M}{P}\right) = L(i - i^m, Y).$$

Here, even though the left-hand side of the equation is invariant with respect to M/P, changing the central bank's interest rate, i^m, can still change the position of the LM curve (i.e., the set of (Y, i) that clear the money market) and have an impact on output and employment. The effect will likely be magnified if the private sector perceives that the central bank does not realize that in a liquidity crisis, with the above-mentioned characteristics, interest rate policy could be significantly more effective than control of monetary aggregates.

Clearly, there are strong parallels between LD and Irving Fisher's debt deflation. Debt deflation arises when bonds or debt are denominated in terms of money/cash and prices fall precipitously, resulting in a sizable increase in the stock of *real* debt (i.e., debt in terms of output) – a situation that reached its climax during the Great Depression (see Fischer (1933)). During the Great Depression wholesale prices fell by about 30 percent, which catapulted the *real* or *output* value of debt to levels that wreaked havoc in the financial sector by generating unplanned overindebtedness, and consequently tended to paralyze credit market *flows* (a phenomenon akin to Sudden Stop). LD is a related phenomenon because our discussion above was also motivated by price deflation, but instead of zeroing in on *solvency*, as in Fischer (1933), it focused on *liquidity*. The question of solvency is not absent because, as prices fall, the output backup of money becomes smaller relative to the stock of *real* monetary balances. Hence the value of money becomes more dependent on its extrinsic liquidity, which may put a limit on the ability of price deflation to generate higher liquidity.

Shadow Banking and International Liquidity Issues

Liquid assets come in different forms and shapes. Cash is the ultimate liquid asset but, as a rule, its nominal (cash) rate of return is nil. Banks are allowed to pay interest on bank deposits, making them strong competitors vis-à-vis cash. However, bank deposits are not safe assets for large clients, like pension funds, because deposit insurance is low relative to their deposits. This poses a problem for banks. Large depositors are keen on holding low-risk deposits because those funds are employed as means of exchange. Absent safe liquid assets that offer attractive rates of return, the lack of deposit insurance would thus call for banks to pile up the asset side of their balance sheets with cash or public debt instruments like Treasury bills.[18] This situation hardly allows banks to offer deals that attract large depositors. Actually large depositors could be better off bypassing banks altogether, and purchasing Treasury bills on their own. This situation became even more challenging for regular banks in the early 2000s, as the Federal Funds rate fell sharply and stayed low for a considerable period of time in response to the dotcom crisis. Arguably, these conditions gave incentives for the creation of Shadow Banks. These banks were able to collateralize their liabilities by investing in ABS.[19] By design (i.e., securitization), ABS are safer than its individual components. Moreover, investing in the upper tranches of these assets, that is, standing first in line for repayment in case of default, can enhance their safety. In addition large deposits are in the form of overnight repo agreements, which further increases the sense of safety since banks would not necessarily go bankrupt if they are subject to a bank run. Under those circumstances the bank still honors the deposit contract by handing over to depositors the assets involved in the repo agreement. There were well-run institutions in place that ensured a low-cost mechanism for the resolution of these claims. Hence repos helped lower bankruptcy costs and ensure quick settlement if shadow banks ran into payments' difficulties, enhancing the liquidity of deposits in shadow banks. Moreover the stability of such systems has been further enhanced in depositors' eyes by the fact that these banks invest in assets that are actively traded in the bond market, and this could have led to the belief that their prices were unlikely to fall in response to problems in *individual* banks. Another factor pushing in the same direction was the very surge of shadow banking, giving rise to what I like to call "inverse bank run" (see below), a *momentum* effect. Finally, the apparent safety of shadow banks could have been reinforced by the popular belief that in case of financial turmoil the Fed would prevent a meltdown of ABS prices (a situation commonly known as the "Fed put"), an instance of "moral hazard." The latter was likely enhanced by the fact that rating agencies got paid by the very ABS issuing financial institutions (e.g., investment banks), another instance of 'moral hazard'. All of these considerations support the view that financial innovation and regulatory agencies policy were major factors behind the significant growth of Shadow Banks.

Impressive as shadow-banking architecture looked prior to crisis, though, these arrangements were not free from a "bad equilibrium." Without a lender of last resort, shadow banks are unable to shield depositors from the consequences of a *systemic* shock in which most of them simultaneously try to withdraw their deposits. This is so despite the fact that, as noted above, these banks need not go bankrupt. They comply with the contract by simply handing over ABS instead of cash. But depositors end up bearing a capital loss as they try to liquidate their ABS holdings. True, on impact wealth redistribution across big players takes place. This needs not have dire output and employment consequences. However, the turmoil involving shadow banks may generate distrust about these institutions, resulting in a credit Sudden Stop (i.e., a large and largely unanticipated fall in credit *flows*). At this juncture Wall Street hits Main Street, causing deleterious outcomes in output and employment. This is in line with events during the 2008 Lehman crisis (see Gorton and Metrick 2012). Chapter 3 will show a simple model bearing out some of these phenomena.

Financial engineering is not the only mechanism for creating liquidity. Higher asset turnover could be enough, as is well documented in the specialized literature (see Foucault et al. 2013). For example, a surge of capital inflows toward EMs could increase EM bonds' liquidity by enlarging their markets, especially during the first stages of a capital-inflow episode in which, perhaps due to heterogeneous investors' expectations, investors do not jump in all at the same time. Under these circumstances, a phenomenon that I call "inverse bank run" (see Calvo 2014a) may take place. To illustrate this phenomenon, suppose new investors enter the EM in a staggered fashion, the best-informed go first, and so on. Thus, before reaching the end of the line, each new entrant knows that there will likely be investors coming after her who are ready to bid for the securities she holds, enhancing the EM bonds' *extrinsic* liquidity. Better informed agents will invest in EM securities, not only on account of those securities' intrinsic rates of return (including expected capital gains) but because the queue behind them makes them to (rationally) expect that it will be easier to liquidate these assets in case informed investors must make, say, an unanticipated cash payment. This increases the incentives of the better informed to purchase the new EM bonds, giving rise to what might look like a rush of depositors eager to cash in their deposits during a bank run—except that in this instance "depositors" are eager to deposit, not withdraw cash from the bank (hence the qualifier adjective "inverse").

Furthermore capital inflows may be stimulated by sizable stocks of international reserves held at the central bank since, as pointed out above, it is reasonable to expect that the latter increases the output anchor of domestic debt instruments. This could conceivably lead to a complex liquidity cycle. For example, a central bank faced with capital inflows triggered by external factors (e.g., QE in DMs) may accumulate international reserves to shield the economy from a potentially larger capital outflow episode. The latter enhances the liquidity of the EM liabilities, further increasing capital inflows—and inducing the central bank to accumulate more reserves, and so on. This may converge to an inefficient equilibrium, which is not necessarily free from Sudden Stop of credit *flows* – because international reserves are implicitly held to protect the *stock* of bank liabilities.

Complementary Notes on the Price Theory of Money

The Price Theory of Money: A Rallying Cry against "Money Causes Prices?

The PTM and extensions discussed here may sound like a rallying cry against the conventional view that "money causes prices" or, recalling Friedman's dictum, "inflation is always and everywhere a monetary phenomenon." But this could not be farthest from the truth. PTM is not saying, "Friedman is dead!" PTM is a theory that helps to explain why cash can survive even under circumstances in which other important liquid assets, such as bank deposits in the 1930s or ABS recently, suffer a major shakeup. The resilience of cash is traced to the fact that a critical number of wages and prices are largely predetermined (sticky) in the short run. This assumption was reasonable at the time of the *General Theory*, because dollar/sterling inflation was not a major issue. The same holds true nowadays in DMs. However, this does not imply that inflation is no longer a relevant consideration. Woodford's (2003) textbook, for instance, shows models displaying staggered prices in which a more lax monetary policy can give rise to higher inflation, in line with Friedman's dictum.

However, inflation may debilitate cash's output anchor. This phenomenon becomes evident during high-inflation episodes. A common market response to high inflation is shortening the duration of price quotations or linking the latter to, say, the exchange rate or some average price level index like the CPI. In the limit, indexation may largely remove cash's role as a mean of exchange (and hence its extrinsic liquidity) by, for example, replacing the local currency by the dollar, a common phenomenon in EMs, and called Currency Substitution (e.g., see Calvo 1996, pt. III).[20]

Nevertheless, high inflation does not eliminate the relevance of the PTM. Even during the record-breaking interwar European hyperinflation episodes, domestic monies kept circulating until they were removed by monetary reform. The realm of these rapidly depreciating units of accounts shrunk but wages continued to be defrayed in terms domestic money. Wages were frequently updated, but some degree of price stickiness prevailed, which might have given incentives to quote prices in terms of domestic money and put in motion the output backup mechanism associated with the PTM.

A Digression on the Keynes/Minsky Discussion of Liquidity Issues

The claim that liquidity is a fundamental factor behind deep financial crises can be traced back to the insightful discussion of liquidity issues in Keynes (1936). Actually the present chapter stands on two golden pillars in the *General Theory*: the Price Theory of Money (Keynes 1936, ch.17) and the Beauty Contest (Keynes (1936, ch. 12), the latter being an example of equilibrium multiplicity. As argued, these two pillars help rationalize the existence of a relatively robust unit of account, while some assets denominated in that unit of account suffer liquidity crunch. Curiously, though, neither the *General Theory*, nor Minsky (2008a, b), who followed on Keynes's footsteps, employ the two pillars to develop a simple and appealing first-approximation rationalization of deep financial crisis and liquidity trap. Keynes (1936), for instance, discusses the Beauty Contest in the context of *long-term expectations,* and although there are some references to equilibrium multiplicity in chapters 17 and 19, the latter is not given a central role there. Instead, Keynes/Minsky discussions wandered into complex territory involving informational imperfections and *pecuniary externalities*. This leads me to wonder if analytical complexity plus the long tranquil macroeconomic environment that prevailed after WWII in developed economies conspired to throw liquidity issues into the trash basket, despite Minsky's later strenuous efforts to refloat them. And, as a result, nourished the twentieth-century naive view (with the benefit of hindsight) that, say, automatic stabilizers and prudent monetary policy are all one needs to defeat the business cycle, particularly deep recession.

A Semantic Note

To some extent, liquidity crunch does involve some sort of "liquidity illusion"—but not the "money illusion" that so worried our ancestors (e.g., see Fisher 2012). Money illusion refers to wrongly assessing the *real* value of money or assets denominated in money, as a consequence of employing a wrong *price level* as a deflator, namely, by selecting the wrong *denominator*. In contrast, *liquidity illusion* is an error in assessing the real value of assets but, in this instance, the error lies in not taking into account potential liquidity crunch, implying that the error is in evaluating the resilience of the *numerator*.

Summary and Implications

1. The liquidity approach helps to rationalize phenomena that would look highly disconcerting if liquidity considerations are not brought to bear. A prominent example is the resilience of the US dollar relative to other liquid assets during the subprime crisis, while other liquid dollar-denominated assets suffered a phenomenal liquidity crunch. Building on Keynes's Price Theory of Money, I claim

that this has much to do with the dollar's prominent role as a global unit of account, linked to nominal stickiness in labor and product markets. Another example is global Sudden Stops. Explanations of the latter that do not rely on liquidity considerations would likely call for a radical revision of the dominant macroeconomic paradigm.

2. A liquidity crunch has effects on relative prices. The nature of these effects depends on which assets suffer the crunch.

3. A natural implication of the PTM is that there may be cases in which an increase in money supply may fail to generate higher liquidity, limiting the effectiveness of monetary policy during periods of liquidity shortage.

4. Moreover, under liquidity deflation, the Pigou effect may stop working. Thus full employment may not be achievable by (1) price deflation, even absent Fisher (1933) debt deflation phenomenon; or (2) expanding money supply, even though prices are sticky.

5. Financial stability is no guarantee against liquidity crunch. The stability of a given arrangement could lead to the false conclusion that risks of financial turmoil are over. This and the previous chapter have argued that extrinsic liquidity may be subject to self-fulfilling shocks that not only harm financial instruments but also end up hurting the real economy. This is not necessarily a consequence of nonrational expectations. Misinformation is enough. The latter is particularly plausible when there is room for multiple equilibriums and the latter are associated with new markets or untested instruments. From this perspective, one could somewhat paradoxically conclude that financial *instability* may help shield the economy from future liquidity crunch episodes—since crisis teaches something that was not well known before it occurred!

6. Safe monies with low rates of return could trigger liquidity bubbles that end up in costly credit Sudden Stop, even under rational expectations.

7. Capital inflows can increase the liquidity of EM liabilities (*inverse bank run*), thereby stimulating further capital inflows. These flows, however, are highly sensitive to a rise in DM policy interest rates. EM monies have weak real anchors. Instead of liquidity trap, they are likely to experience sharp currency devaluation during liquidity crunch. Moreover the exchange rate could become highly volatile even under normal conditions.

8. The liquidity approach does not offer easy solutions for policy makers but should open their eyes to risks that were largely ignored by mainstream macroeconomics until the subprime crisis—and are unlikely to go away in the near future.

This chapter has focused on understanding financial crises. But one should not dismiss the positive role of a well output-anchored fiat money or equivalent asset in terms of which prices and wages are quoted. A lack of this kind of instrument might seriously impair the functioning of trade and credit markets. Thus, in a way, liquidity is both a blessing and a curse of modern capitalist economies.

3 Monetary Theory: Overview and Liquidity Extensions

Money, banking and finance cannot be understood unless allowance is made for financial evolution and innovation: money, in truth, is an endogenously determined variable—the supply is responsive to demand and not something mechanically controlled by the Federal Reserve.

Minsky (2008a, p. 252)

The objective of this chapter is to highlight some key aspects of mainstream monetary theory, pointing out its glaring limitations to guide policy under liquidity turmoil, but showing that the theory can easily be modified to provide some clues on the impact of liquidity crunch. The models discussed here are simple and, as most current financial crisis models, assume that liquidity shocks are exogenous.

The chapter starts with a discussion of mainstream monetary theory—more specifically a barebones version of the New Keynesian model employed in many central banks. It proceeds to modify the model to account for liquidity factors and get new and interesting insights. The chapter also discusses the limitations of the Fiscal Theory of the Price Level under liquidity crunch conditions, and presents a critique of some aspects of the new crop of financial crisis models.

Modeling "Money": Some Basic Issues

"Money" has always been at the center of macroeconomic debates, especially debates dealing with short-run issues. For a long time money was kept separate from the theory of value. Relative prices were assumed to be determined by demand and supply forces that ignored money. The price level was assumed determined by the equality of money demand and supply, taking output and relative prices as given. Irving Fisher (1912) offers a classic exposition of this approach. His book does not ignore links with the real economy, but these issues are overshadowed by discussions about the velocity of circulation of money. Keynes (1936) questions the separation between money and the theory of value, but the first systematic integration of these two branches of economic theory had to await Patinkin (1965).[1]

Typically, monetary theory assumes that the main functions of money are as a *unit of account*, a *means of exchange* (MOE) and a *store of value*. The canonical model following Patinkin (1965) assumes that the economy operates in full autarky (*closed-economy* case) and is endowed with only one type of fiat money. This model was extended to open economies, but in most cases money was assumed to have a local role, except for a few monies like the US dollar that were assumed to be held by central banks as international reserves—but not held by private agents outside the countries of issue.[2] A salient characteristic of these models is that money is introduced as a *deus ex machina* with weak microfoundations and, more relevant for our discussion here, without taking into account that in a realistic economy there are a variety of externally liquid assets (recall definition in chapter 2), in addition to money. These models ignore the PTM and make assumptions such as that money has a positive value in terms of output, and the demand for money function is smooth (typically continuous and twice-continuously differentiable in mathematical models).[3]

The basic structure of the canonical model has endured until today, although it has been subject to many modifications and extensions. One extension, in particular, stands up: rational expectations (RE). This is a controversial assumption but, in one way or another, still lies at the heart of most models currently employed by central banks. If the central bank is confident about the basic structure of the model, the RE assumption allows the analyst to infer the inflation path that would be consistent with the model and policy rules, *provided that the public trusts the central bank's announcements.* This does not require the private sector to know the model or to be rational in the sense of the RE literature. For this modeling strategy to be useful for monetary policy, it is critical that the central bank enjoys a great deal of *credibility.* More concretely, the central bank has to succeed in making its inflation forecasts credible to the private sector. This is the most important condition for the applicability of these models.

However, the RE literature also shows that credibility cannot be taken for granted. There are fundamental reasons for policy makers *not to be credible* because, as a rule, policy makers have incentives to behave in a *time-inconsistent* manner, that is, depart from previous policy announcements, even though they are not "cheaters" and are exclusively interested in trying to maximize social welfare (see Kydland and Prescott 1977; Calvo 1978). Moreover credibility problems can get exacerbated in the midst of a financial crisis when, in addition to the incentive-compatibility issues highlighted by the time-inconsistency literature, central banks face the possibility of equilibrium multiplicity driven by liquidity crunch (an issue raised in chapter 2). Thus it is worrisome that credibility issues are given little weight, if at all, in models employed by central banks and in the new generation of post-crisis models. This and other weaknesses will become more apparent after spelling out a barebones' version of central banks' rational expectations model.

A Barebones Central Bank Rational Expectations Model

The model, which is a version of the New Keynesian approach, can be expressed in terms of the following four equations:

$$i = r + \pi, \tag{1}$$

$$\frac{\dot{c}}{c} = r - \rho, \tag{2}$$

$$\dot{\pi} = \bar{y} - c, \tag{3}$$

and

$$i = r + \bar{\pi} + \alpha(\pi - \bar{\pi}) + \beta(c - \bar{y}); \quad \alpha, \beta > 0, \tag{4}$$

where $i, r, \pi, c, \rho, \bar{y}$, and $\bar{\pi}$ stand for nominal and real interest rate, inflation, consumption, (constant) subjective rate of discount, (constant) full-employment output, and (constant) target inflation, respectively; a dot on a variable denotes the variable's derivative with respect to time; time subscripts are dropped for simplicity. This is a continuous-time perfect-foresight model. Equation (1) is Fisher's equation, equating the nominal interest rate i to the real interest rate r plus the expected rate of inflation π; equation (2) is the Euler equation or modern IS curve (assuming log utility); equation (3) is a simplified form of Calvo (1983) staggered prices; and equation (4) is the central bank rule. Except for α and β, all other usual parameters have been set equal to 1 to simplify the notation. Under these assumptions, it can easily be shown that the system boils down to two differential equations in c and π; these variables are free to take any initial value, subject to c being non-negative. If Taylor rule's interest rates condition holds (i.e., $\beta > 1$), and $\alpha > 0$, *no matter how small*, the two characteristics roots have positive real parts. Hence the steady state is the only *locally converging* path. Consequently, if *local* path convergence is a condition that RE paths must satisfy (a condition imposed in DSGE models, although not unanimously endorsed in the literature, see Cochrane 2011), the system exhibits a unique equilibrium, which in this case coincides with the steady state.

This type of model has, of course, been extended in different directions. However, the following comments in the light of the discussion in previous chapters apply to most of them:

1. The model succeeds in giving a rationale to the common central bank practice (especially in DMs under normal conditions) of utilizing the rate of interest as a central instrument for monetary policy, and downplays variables like exchange rates and monetary aggregates. Prior to the development of New Keynesian models, the conventional wisdom was that the interest rate (being essentially a relative price) was not enough to determine the price level, especially under rational expectations. The New Keynesian innovation was to assume staggered sticky prices, and rule out "explosive" paths as equilibrium candidates. The sticky prices assumption is more controversial and will be discussed below—but it is supported by empirical evidence. Notice that sticky prices provide a nominal anchor and, at the same time, are the main friction that prevents the system from being at full employment/capacity at all times. This is

an example of market failure that, according to the model, the central bank can help to mitigate. The New Keynesian literature, though, missed the Price Theory of Money discussed above. In it, price stickiness plays an even more fundamental central role: it helps provide an output anchor to *money as a unit of account.*

2. Liquidity issues are completely swept under the rug. Money supply, for instance, does not show up explicitly in the model because the central bank sets its policy interest rate i and lets money supply be demand determined. Moreover, although assets associated with i are highly liquid, Fisher equation (1)—bereft of liquidity considerations—is assumed to hold. Fortunately, however, if the model is extended to account for the liquidity of assets associated with central bank policy interest rate, monetary policy is effective, even if the Taylor rule does not hold, that is, $\beta < 1$. However, the price level determination requires control of a stock of liquid assets. The latter includes standard money aggregates, like M_2 but also, as a general rule, a much wider set of assets, several of which are not controlled by the central bank. Under this lens, policy interest rates recede into the background, while "aggregates" once again take center stage. The main challenge is that these aggregates may be much harder to control than standard money aggregates, especially in sophisticated financial markets. See chapter 4.

3. Equation (2) implies that there are no major debt or financial problems that interfere with intertemporal trade. In particular, the role of liquidity in capital markets is completely obliterated.

4. The model has nothing to say about bubbles, especially bubbles generated by low policy interest rates, an issue highlighted in chapter 2, and discussed below.

5. As noted above, central bank credibility cannot be taken for granted, especially in crisis situations. This was not an important issue in DMs until recently, but ignoring it under the present conditions could be a serious omission. There is ample evidence and theory pointing out to the fact that imperfect policy credibility can yield costly results. This issue got a lot of attention in regard with a number of failed EM inflation stabilization programs (e.g., see Calvo and Végh 1999; Buffie and Manoj Atolia 2012).

6. Excluding divergent equilibrium paths—a common practice in the RE literature—is questionable,[4] especially if the Taylor rule is adopted. Take, for instance, a path that satisfies equations (1) to (4) but follows a hyperinflation trajectory. Taylor rule implies that the *real* interest rate r must grow without bound. This is likely to have severe consequences on the real sector (including highly regressive income redistribution), and may lead the public to expect that the Taylor rule will be dropped. The possibility of a *policy switch* along potentially explosive paths may give rise to converging equilibriums other than the steady state (in the model above).[5] Moreover, even if policy makers are expected to stick to Taylor's rule (4), equilibrium indeterminacy might still hold. This would be the case, for instance, if the negative effect of the real interest rate r on full-employment output $\bar{y}$ is large enough. See below for a proof.

7. Finally, a criticism that applies to virtually all models with a representative individual and rational expectations is that the welfare costs of suboptimal monetary policy— measured by the equivalent consumption loss on the basis of the model—are, as a general rule, insignificant—unless they generate effects that are not explicitly contemplated in most central bank models, such as growth deceleration,

equilibrium multiplicity, or very high volatility.[6] Therefore, despite the admittedly intellectual achievement behind these models, one is led to conclude that their insights on optimal monetary policy are "irrelevant" when conditions are such that the models are applicable—and, of course, even more so when they are not![7]

The Fiscal Theory of the Price Level (FTPL): A Digression
The FTPL shows that determination of the price level can be ensured *even though* two popular monetary anchors, namely money supply and exchange rate, are endogenous and market-determined—not set by policy. In particular, in a closed-economy context, the FTPL shows that price level determination could hold if the central bank targets the nominal interest rate and lets money supply be fully demand-determined. At first, this result may sound implausible because the nominal interest rate is an index of the *relative* price of money *today* in terms of money *tomorrow*, not an *absolute* price, that is, a price in terms of money. To illustrate, consider the following demand for money,

$$\frac{M}{P} = L(i),$$

where M, P, and i denote, respectively, money supply, the price level, and the nominal interest rate. Under interest-rate targeting the central bank sets the nominal interest rate i while letting M and P be market-determined. Let ζ be such that $\zeta = L(\bar{i})$, where $\bar{i}$ denotes the central bank's interest-rate target. Hence it can easily be verified in a standard model that any vector (M, P) such that $M/P = \zeta$ is consistent with general equilibrium, and therefore money supply and the price level are indeterminate.

The FTPL literature points out that the result above relies on assuming that fiscal policy is endogenous and adjusts to the needs imposed by monetary policy. If, however, fiscal policy is unresponsive to monetary policy, this is equivalent to introducing additional constraints that, in some cases, help pin down the price level. The literature has focused on the government's budget constraint (e.g., see Leeper 1991; Woodford 1995). To illustrate how price determination might take effect if fiscal policy is unresponsive (or "active" according Leeper's 1991 definition), consider the simple example discussed in Christiano and Fitzgerald (2000). The government's budget constraint takes the following form:

$$\frac{\kappa B}{P} = \text{present value of future fiscal } real \text{ primary surpluses,}$$

where κ is a parameter to be discussed shortly, and B stands for the present stock of *nominal* government debt, a predetermined variable at *present*. Thus, if one assumes that the right-hand side of the equation above is predetermined, the equation determines the price level P. No reference to the money market equilibrium is necessary. In the standard discussion $\kappa = 1$. This sounds plausible under "normal" circumstances because if $\kappa = 1$, the equation implies that the government will pay the outstanding debt with future fiscal surpluses.

However, active fiscal policy is a more controversial assumption during financial crises, our focus here. One feature missing from the standard FTPL is *debt default*. Debt default, in some form or another, has been a ubiquitous feature in financial crises. Salient examples are the Brady plan associated with the 1980s debt crisis in less-developed economies, the current Greece crisis, and a good number of episodes in developed market economies where debt default, sometimes involving disingenuous procedures, reached record levels (e.g., see Reinhart and Sbrancia 2011; Reinhart and Trebesh 2014). Thus, in terms of the equation above, the possibility of debt default is equivalent to saying that in financial crisis episodes, κ adjusts and fiscal policy becomes 'passive' (in Leeper's 1991 terminology).[8]

Another relevant phenomenon ignored by the FTPL is *liquidity*. As argued in preceding chapters, *liquidity* of financial assets played a key role in financial crises—the subprime crisis offering the most telling global example of the last seventy years. Liquidity is a complex concept, but fortunately, one can get an inkling of its implications for the FTPL by linking parameter κ to liquidity. In the conventional FTPL model, government bonds B are assumed to provide no liquidity services that are comparable to those obtained through money M. Therefore, ruling out default, it is plausible to assume $\kappa = 1$. To help develop intuition, consider the polar opposite case in which government debt provides the same liquidity services as money. Money is a type of government debt that, in an infinite horizon model needs never be paid back. Hence, in that special case, $\kappa = 0$, and the FTPL nominal anchor would be entirely lost. More realistically, let us introduce parameter θ, which will play a central role later in this chapter. I define θ as the share of public debt B that is endowed with money-like liquidity. Under this interpretation, one could set $\kappa = 1 - \theta$, since θB needs never be repaid. To illustrate, consider the liquidity trap that occurred in the Lehman crisis, and discussed in chapter 2. This could be interpreted as a flight to public sector debt B provoked by a rise in its liquidity coefficient θ (implying a drop in κ). If fiscal policy is fully "active," and the liquidity shock is taken as a *money market* shock to which fiscal authorities are not supposed to react—the price level would have to fall (i.e., deflation would set in) giving rise to Fisherian debt deflation. This may drive fiscal authorities to lower the right-hand side of the equation above (i.e., increase future fiscal deficits, as the US government did after the Lehman crisis), making fiscal policy passive.[9]

Consequently price level determination and inflation in times of crisis are unlikely to be firmly pinned down by FTPL considerations. Moreover the credibility and equilibrium indeterminacy issues raised above in connection with the barebones central bank model also besiege the FTPL.

Accounting for Liquidity Effects: Demand Side

I will now illustrate some relevant effects that can easily be rationalized by including liquidity considerations in standard models. I will start by extending the previous model in order to account for assets other than money that provide liquidity services. Calvo and Végh (1995) accomplishes this for the case in which Treasury bills or bank deposits are money substitutes. Here I will assume that *land* provides liquidity services. This is motivated by asset-backed securities, early examples of which are mortgage-backed securities that have played a central role in the subprime crisis.

Let us assume the existence of a representative individual whose utility function can be expressed as follows:

$$\int_0^\infty [u(c_t) + v(m_t + \theta q_t k_t)]e^{-\rho t}dt, \tag{5}$$

where $m, k,$ and q are, respectively, real monetary balances, stock of land and its price in terms of output (= consumption). Functions u and v are strictly increasing and concave. In conventional models parameter $\theta = 0$. Assuming $1 > \theta > 0$ is equivalent to saying that land is a means of exchange inferior to money; its "moneyness" or liquidity is proportional to the market value of land, that is, qk. This assumption is explored at length in Calvo (2012b). By utility function (5), the real value of liquidity held by the representative consumer is equal to $m_t + q_t k_t$. Hence its output opportunity cost is given by

$$r_t(m_t + q_t k_t),\tag{6}$$

where, as in previous model, r denotes the real interest rate (i.e., the output or consumption own rate of interest on assets that do not yield liquidity services). In line with Calvo and Végh (1995) and Calvo (2012b), I will assume that the central bank pays interest on money at the rate i^m, and identify the latter with the policy interest rate. Therefore the real yield on money is $i^m - \pi$. Now, in contrast, assuming that the marginal productivity of land is constant and, without loss of generality, equal to ρ, the real yield on land is $\rho + \dot{q}$, where $\dot{q}$ stands for the expected real capital gains from holding a unit of land. Therefore, recalling expression (6), the net cost of holding m and k is given by the following expression (where time subscripts are omitted for simplicity):

$$(r + \pi - i^m)m + (rq - \rho - \dot{q})k.\tag{7}$$

By (5), total liquidity held in the hands of the representative individual equals

$$l \equiv m + \theta q k.\tag{8}$$

Given l, the individual minimizes the cost of holding money and land or, more formally, minimizes (7) subject to (8), given l. It trivially follows that at interior solutions the following equality must hold:

$$q = \frac{\rho + \dot{q}}{r - \theta(r + \pi - i^m)}.\tag{9}$$

Consider the special case in which $r = \rho$, and $\pi = i^m = \dot{q} = 0$. Then, by (9),

$$q = \frac{1}{1-\theta}. \tag{9'}$$

Thus, under the standard assumption that money is the only source of liquidity services, that is, $\theta = 0$, we have $q = 1$. Moreover the price of land increases with its liquidity coefficient θ.[10] However, as pointed out in chapter 2, θ is a coefficient that depends on the intrinsic and extrinsic liquidity of land. A run on MBS (i.e., a fall in θ), for instance, of the sort that took place during the Lehman crisis, results in a meltdown in real estate prices (here q). In a richer model, securitization involved in the architecture of MBS is likely to imbue these assets with *extrinsic liquidity*, a phenomenon that, as discussed above, depends more on social implicit compacts than land pledgeability—and hence opens up the possibility of an *across-the-board* fall in θ. This is worth highlighting because, as discussed at the end of this section, if only *intrinsic liquidity* was involved in θ, its sudden fall would require assuming that the share of land holdings in an economy that can be pledged will exhibit a large and sudden collapse. This may hold true in a social revolution, but it is not what happens in regular financial crises.

The more general equation (9) reveals a set of interesting results. First, the price of land increases as the policy interest rate declines. The intuition is straightforward, since as i^m falls, land becomes more attractive than money as a medium of exchange. This effect depends on land offering liquidity services. If $\theta = 0$, a fall in i^m would have no effect on q. Second, a rise in expected inflation could succeed in lifting q—but, again, only if land is endowed with liquidity, that is, $\theta > 0$. Third, in line with standard theory, a decline in the real interest rate r has a positive effect on the price of land. This effect holds true even in the case in which $\theta = 0$, as expected.

The model discussed here is static and does not address the case in which liquidity rises gradually over time. This would be the case in the inverse bank run scenario discussed in chapter 2, for example. Under those circumstances, the price of land could be expected to increase over time, that is, $\dot{q} > 0$, which, by equation (9), would put additional upward pressure on land prices.

This simple example shows that liquidity creation collateralized by real assets can have an effect on those assets' *relative* price. This is in sharp contrast with the conventional monetary model in which money is the only liquid asset and is "neutral," which is to say, that under price flexibility a once-and-for-all change in the quantity of money has no effect on relative prices. Money neutrality still holds in the present model because at steady state the stock of money has *no* effect on the price of land q. However, a run on MBS (a fall in liquidity coefficient θ), for example, leading to a meltdown on real estate *relative* prices may not be offset by an aggressive increase in liquidity geared exclusively on expanding money supply.

In chapter 2 I discussed the possibility that liquidity may be endogenously determined by variables like the policy interest rate i^m. The model can be extended by assuming that increasing the liquidity of land is possible but costly, and that a lower i^m gives rise to a higher θ and, by equation (9′), to a higher price of land q. The reader can find a formal discussion about this issue in Calvo (2012b). The endogenous-liquidity discussion offers a rationale for the statement that the Fed's low-interest-rate policy is partly responsible for the surge in real estate prices prior to the subprime crisis. The statement is not new and has been put forward by the Fed's critics. However, the typical critics' argument relies on a conventional effect that does not distinguish between the interest rate on liquid and nonliquid assets. Critics probably identify the relevant interest rate with r in the above model, not i^m. But, if this is true, how does one explain the burst of the bubble in the Lehman crisis despite the aggressively much lower interest rates engineered by the Fed (recall chapter 1, figure 1.3)? In contrast, the liquidity explanation offers a rationale that is more in line with the facts. One could argue that the lengthy period of low interest rates (i.e., low i^m) induced the financial sector to improve the *extrinsic* liquidity of assets associated with "land," increasing its price, as argued above. The sharp increase in interest rates produced the opposite effect. One could also argue that lowering rates after the bubble burst were not effective because pricking a liquidity bubble brings about financial disruption that cannot be removed by a mere lowering of interest rates. This would be the case if a fall in real estate relative prices brought about by liquidity crunch gave rise to a slew of bankruptcies that could not be speedily dealt by the courts (a *congestion* effect).

A key insight of the example is that financial engineering can change relative prices. Whether this is enough to rationalize, say, the recent real estate bubble is indeed an open question. But even if financial engineering falls short of the mark, the fact that developments in the financial sector can have an effect on relative prices can put in motion other factors that magnify the initial impact from financial engineering. Yet, a more satisfactory model would spell out the factors behind the collapse in θ. I will not discuss this issue here, but note that, in principle, this type of collapse has nothing mysterious about it. As discussed in preceding chapters, it is almost a defining characteristic of liquidity, especially extrinsic liquidity. Moreover Morris and Shin (1998) present a very elegant model in which equilibrium multiplicity holds when individuals share common information, but uniqueness is restored if individuals base their expectation on disparate information sources. The model could easily be adapted to the case in which θ is subject to runs. However, this analytical "trick" would be of little comfort to the policy maker. From the policy maker's point of view, the "equilibrium multiplicity" problem does not go away because, even if uniqueness holds, Morris and Shin (1998) show that the equilibrium solution is sensitive to parameters that are likely to be hidden from the view of the policy maker. In summary: From a policy maker's point of view, liquid assets are a potential source of severe *systemic* volatility, even if uniqueness could be guaranteed!

Accounting for Liquidity Effects: Supply Side

A standard assumption in monetary models is that money enters the utility function as in equation (5) and is held by households. However, liquidity is also important for firms and banks, and for other sectors of the economy. A simple way to take account of this phenomenon is to include money is production functions. Examples are as follows:

• Fischer (1974), Levhari and Patinkin (1968), and Calvo (1979), which assume that money is a factor of production, and
• Stockman (1981), which assumes that investment is subject to a cash-in-advance constraint; that is, firms

planning to invest must hold a proportional amount of money during a nonnegligible period of time.

This subsection will highlight some unconventional and relevant implications of this approach.

Suppose that full-capacity output $\bar{y} = f(m)$, m = real monetary balances. Function f is increasing, strictly concave (and continuously differentiable). Profit maximization implies that the firm maximizes

$$f(m) - im,$$

with respect m, where i is the nominal interest rate, identified as the opportunity cost of holding real monetary balances. Hence, at interior solutions, the following first-order condition holds:

$$f'(m) = i.$$

Full-capacity output is a negative function of i, in that there exists a function $\varnothing(i)$, such that at equilibrium

$$\bar{y} = \varnothing(i), \quad \varnothing' < 0. \tag{10}$$

Therefore, in contrast with the IS/LM framework, an increase in the expected rate of inflation (raising i) would have a negative effect on full-capacity output. Thus, even though, below full capacity, inflation could provide some stimulus to output and employment, equation (10) implies that the inflation medicine may encounter a lower output ceiling than if output expansion was associated with low inflation. Observers that do not take this into account will see inflation rising and output falling before reaching (what they would continue to call) full employment, namely the nasty cocktail that characterizes stagflation (see Friedman 1977 for similar arguments).

Liquidity effects can be easily added to the model. For example, one could assume $\bar{y} = f(\theta m)$, where θ is the liquidity coefficient. Thus, a fall in θ implies output contraction. There are many other variants around this theme. The likelihood of a large fall in θ depends on the nature of the liquid assets involved in variable m. If m is largely fiat money, for instance, the Price Theory of Money suggests that a fall in θ is less of an issue.[11] However, it is unlikely that firms' liquidity take only the form of fiat money (or assets protected by a lender of last resort). These alternative assets are typically denominated in terms of fiat money and involve medium or long-term commitments (e.g., long-maturity constant nominal coupon bonds). In a stochastic environment, the external liquidity of the latter may be a negative function of the rate of inflation because inflation volatility tends to be positively correlated with expected inflation.[12]

Another example is Stockman (1981). In Stockman's model money does not enter the production function but investment is assumed to be subject to a cash-in-advance condition in a full-employment context.[13] Stockman shows that an increase in the rate of inflation lowers the rate of growth, a result that runs counter to the then popular conjecture that moderate inflation stimulates growth (see Tobin 1965). One simple way to capture the intuition in Stockman (1981) is to assume a discrete-time model in which output is produced by intermediate inputs x and that the production function is $\bar{y} = g(x)$, where g satisfies all the regularity condition of function f above. Output is homogeneous, and thus the relative price of x with respect to $\bar{y}$ equals 1. The cash-in-advance constraint takes the following form (for simplicity, $\bar{y}$, x, and m are contemporaneous variables)

$x = m.$

Therefore the profit function is given by

$$f(x) - (1+i)x.$$

Maximization with respect to x implies, at an interior optimum, recalling equation (1),

$$f'(x) = 1 + i = 1 + r + \pi, \tag{11}$$

where, again, r and π stand for the real interest rate and expected inflation. This result is equivalent to equation (10): full-employment output declines with the nominal interest rate. At a steady state, for example, in which the real interest rate equals the subjective rate of discount, it follows that an increase in the expected rate of inflation lowers output.

The model in Stockman (1981) is dynamic because production is assumed to depend on physical putty-putty capital, and investment is subject to a cash-in-advance constraint. However, the steady-state implications of Stockman's richer model are the same as above: steady-state output falls with inflation.

I will now go back to the central bank's barebones model discussed above, and stick $\varnothing(i)$ in lieu of $\bar{y}$ in equations (1) to (4). It can be shown that if $\varnothing'(i)$ is large enough in absolute value, there exists a continuum of equilibrium paths converging to the steady state. This is so because, evaluated at steady state, there would be two real characteristic roots of opposite signs, giving rise to a saddle-path configuration. These conditions do not invalidate the central bank's model for policy guidance, but they open up the possibility that the economy travels along other local equilibrium solutions, which is to say, equilibrium multiplicity prevails.[14]

In summary, supply-side liquidity effects help to rationalize phenomena like stagflation, and output slump as a result of, for instance, a meltdown in asset-backed securities—features that are absent from models that high-light demand-side liquidity shocks. Chapter 5 will combine these two types of effects in a model that is able to make liquidity crunch with liquidity trap—two salient phenomena in the Lehman crisis—mutually compatible.

Banks and Credit

Extensions to account for banks and credit are straightfor-ward. One can modify the demand-side liquidity model by assuming that banks' non-capital funding consists of depos-its and are subject to a liquidity constraint. Banks extend loans to firms for the acquisition of land k through mortgage-backed securities. Once again, the output value of land is denoted by q. Banks can hold liquidity in the form of cash, m, or mortgage-backed securities, qk, and they are allowed to lend the rest in terms of illiquid bonds; see the T-account in table 3.1.

Denoting the liquidity requirement by δ, $0 < \delta < 1$, bank liquidity requirement satisfies

$$\text{bank liquidity} = m + \theta qk = \delta d. \tag{12}$$

For simplicity, I will focus on the special case in which $r = \rho$, and $\pi = i^m = \dot{q} = 0$. Since the production function is rk, at a competitive equilibrium the following zero-profit condi-tion must hold:

Table 3.1

	Bank assets	Bank liabilities
	m	d = deposits
Liquid assets	qk = mortgage-backed securities	bank capital
	x = noncollateralized loans (interest rate = r)	

$$rk - sqk = 0, \tag{13}$$

where s is the interest rate on infinite-horizon or no-maturity mortgages. The opportunity cost of holding liquidity is

$$r(m + qk) - sqk = r(\delta d - \theta qk) + (r - s)qk, \tag{14}$$

where the left-hand expression is akin to expression (7) above under the special assumptions made here (recall paragraph below equation 12); and the right-hand side expression takes account of liquidity constraint (12). Hence, at an interior optimum, cost minimization of liquidity holding implies that

$$s = r(1 - \theta), \tag{15}$$

which, combined with equation (13), yields equation (9'). The general equilibrium model considered in the demand-side discussion could be modified by assuming that consumers hold liquidity in the form of bank deposits d, and the utility index in expression (5) becomes $v(d)$, where d is expressed in terms of output. Note that the net rate of return on land and x are equalized. A switch from land to non-land loans per unit of land loan results in a loss of the mortgage return, s, and a net gain of $r(1 - \delta)$, because non-land loans earn a gross return equal to r but require a liquidity provision equal to δ, per unit of loan. Equality follows from equation (15).

The demand-side model exhibits no output effect, but the latter can be easily appended. One possibility is to assume that we are looking at a steady state in which landowners have acquired land on a mortgage, and that qk in the banks' balance sheet above is the market value of those mortgages. Thus, a fall in land's liquidity (i.e., a fall in θ) results in a decline in the price of land, a capital loss for firms that can be transferred to banks by filing for bankruptcy. This may cause a Diamond–Dybvig (1983)-type bank run, which interrupts credit flows, and so on. Another, more conventional extension is, for instance, to assume that k stands for putty-putty neoclassical capital, such that the price of capital in terms of output $q = 1$.

$$\text{bank liquidity} = m + \theta k = \delta d. \tag{12'}$$

Interior solutions for the cost-minimization problem faced by banks still call for equation (15) to hold (i.e., $s = r(1-\theta)$). Let $f(k)$ be a regular neoclassical production function. Hence profit maximization calls for setting

$$f'(k) = s = r(1-\theta). \tag{16}$$

Consider the steady state of this economy where the pure real rate of interest $r = \rho =$ the subjective rate of discount. Then, a fall in land's liquidity (i.e., a fall in θ) lowers steady-state capital.[15]

Monetary Theory in Times of Crisis: A Critical Assessment

The preceding remarks show that some basic liquidity issues can be accommodated in terms of conventional monetary models. The extensions discussed here focus on "essentials." Yet, they open perspectives about the effect of monetary policy that differ in interesting and useful ways from the conventional model presented at the outset. These extensions help illustrate that if liquidity involves assets beyond standard money, monetary policy may face new challenges that, among other things, require central banks to play close attention to financial variables. However, the extensions do not overcome some of the criticisms raised against the conventional model. The liquidity extensions add a new coefficient/variable, θ, which measures extrinsic liquidity in real assets (*land* in the first example). Whether or not θ is taken as a parameter or made a function of standard variables like interest rates, as in Calvo (2012a), the model is almost identical to the conventional one, and shares some important weaknesses (e.g., items 5 and 6 in the list above). In particular, it fails to tell a satisfactory story for situations in which θ rises, say, and then falls precipitously—a trademark of boom–bust liquidity crises. The discussion above gives some hints that could help to address this issue, but there still is a long road before reaching final destination. The gap is not due to the simplicity of the models. Even much better structured models, like those discussed in Holmström and Tirole (2011), for instance, exhibit this sort of gap.[16]

A popular approach that aims at explaining large swings in credit as a result of liquidity considerations, and is prima facie free from *deus ex machina* tricks, relies on assuming quantitatively relevant *nonlinearities* (these models are commonly categorized as being "highly nonlinear"). This is typically achieved by assuming the existence of pecuniary externalities and, more crucially, of *discontinuous* quantitative constraints. A popular assumption in this regard is that borrowers are subject to well-defined quantitative upper bounds to total indebtedness.[17] This is a realistic assumption because it is not unusual for regulations to make it onerous for banks to extend credit beyond a well-defined share of borrowers' net equity. However, for these models to have a "punch," a *sizable share of economic agents must encounter the borrowing constraint at about the same time*. This feature holds because these models assume the existence of a limited number of different individuals (e.g., informed and uninformed, skillful and unskillful). Thus, for example, in a representative-individual model every single agent hits the borrowing constraint at the same time![18] This type of simultaneity could be realistic if the shock hits too-big-to-fail institutions or the central bank (as in Krugman 1979), for example. However, the bulk of the current crop of papers, especially those dealing with monetary phenomena, assumes the existence of atomistic agents subject to pecuniary externalities. Thus the appeal of these nonlinear models would be greatly enhanced if the model allows for a continuous distribution of agents subject to a variety of liquidity constraints.[19] The "atomicity" assumption, it should be noted, cannot be entirely dispensed with because, otherwise, large agents will internalize those shocks and pecuniary externalities would be hard to justify.

The liquidity approach's modeling of liquidity crunch pursued in this book bears the flavor of the new crop of nonlinear models, especially if, as argued above, uniqueness is ensured by making Morris–Shin (1998) type assumptions. Under those circumstances, a slight shock could have large effects, even in a linear model, because the patched-up model comes from models displaying equilibrium *indeterminacy*, an essential characteristic of *extrinsic liquidity*. This may be more realistic than the available nonlinear models in which the source of nonlinearity is no mystery, and should be easily grasped by policymakers. If, for example, the source of nonlinearity is a regulation that keeps banks from lending beyond a critical loan-to-equity ratio, regulators could solve the problem by "smoothing out" the edges of lending constraints. This type of solution sounds deceivingly simple given the complexity and variety of recent liquidity crises.

4 Nominal Anchoring with Liquid Monetary Policy Assets

Taylor's Principle and Total Liquidity

The flight to safety associated with the current crisis has prompted central banks to turn to unconventional policies like quantitative easing. This policy was adopted as central bank interest rates virtually hit the zero bound while deflationary pressures were far from subsiding. At that juncture, in the United States interest rates on public bonds, for example, were so low that the dividing line between public bonds and high-powered money became exceedingly blurry. This situation is very different from what is assumed in popular monetary models employed by central banks (see previous chapter). In those models, the central bank is assumed to control an interest rate on a financial instrument devoid of liquidity services.[1]

Therefore it has become imperative to have a better understanding about monetary policy in a context in which some types of bonds, such as Treasury bills and MBS, can provide liquidity services. One basic question is whether the existence of liquid bonds impairs or facilitates the effectiveness of monetary policy. In particular, whether interest rate policies are able to provide a nominal anchor by either ensuring uniqueness of the price level, in flexible-price models, or the inflation rate, under price stickiness. As pointed out in chapter 3, equilibrium *uniqueness* is a preeminent condition, without which the central bank could not prevent wild and highly costly volatility. In several papers, Carlos Végh and I have partially addressed this issue by showing that liquid bonds can ensure the existence of a nominal anchor even if the policy interest rate is constant over time, and does not react to the rate of inflation (a policy usually called "interest-rate targeting").[2] This line of research has recently been extended in different interesting directions in Canzoneri and Diba (2005) and Canzoneri et al. (2008).[3]

In this chapter I focus on a purely monetary model under perfect foresight in which any fiscal deficit or surplus associated with monetary policy is offset by lump-sum taxes or subsidies. Thus the analysis is independent of the fiscal theory of the price level. I will examine both cases in which prices are perfectly flexible and in which prices are set in a staggered fashion as in Calvo (1983). By sharply focusing on monetary issues, I will prove general results (not just numerical examples) that may open roads into more realistic scenarios.

The analysis will focus on a slight extension of the barebones model discussed in previous chapter; corner solutions will be ignored, and unstable paths will be ruled out as equilibrium candidates. These strong assumptions with which I do not feel fully comfortable do nevertheless help establish contact with the models that still hold sway in the profession even after the subprime crisis. Since the implications of the model discussed here are radically different from those models, they help highlight the relevance of taking liquidity considerations into account.

One interesting result is that, while liquid bonds ensure that interest-rate targeting yields a unique equilibrium under flexible prices, an interest-rate rule that satisfies the Taylor principle (by which a 1 percent increase in expected inflation is followed by an increase of more than 1 percent in the policy interest rate) can leave the economy without a nominal anchor.[4] Yet, confirming and extending previous work in this area, any rule tying the policy interest rate to inflation under staggered prices provides an inflation anchor, whether or not the Taylor principle is satisfied.[5] If staggered prices are deemed the more realistic scenario, this result is reassuring, since the monetary authority could employ the policy interest rate for other purposes (e.g., financial stability), without necessarily losing the monetary anchor.

Flexible Prices

Suppose a perfect-foresight monetary economy with homogeneous endowment output and perfectly flexible prices. There is a representative individual, whose utility function satisfies

$$\int_0^\infty [u(c_t) + v(m_t) + h(b_t)]e^{-\rho t}dt, \tag{1}$$

where 0 stands for present time; c, m, b stand for consumption, real monetary, and externally liquid bond balances, respectively; and ρ stands for the positive and constant subjective rate of discount. Functions u, v, and h are twice continuously differentiable, strictly increasing, and concave on the positive real line. The new unconventional assumption is that extrinsically liquid bonds (e.g., Treasury bills), which are directly or indirectly employed for monetary policy, are endowed with liquidity.[6]

At any point in time, the representative individual's backward-looking wealth in real terms, w, satisfies

$$w_t = m_t + b_t + x_t, \tag{2}$$

where x is a pure bond, devoid of liquidity services, that individuals employ to borrow and lend among themselves. Since in this setup individuals are assumed to be identical in all respects, in equilibrium $x = 0$ for all t. However, introducing it in the analysis allows Lagrange multipliers to be used instead of more sophisticated Pontryagin's techniques. The nominal rate of interest on x and b are denoted by i and s, respectively. Variable s will be identified with the *policy interest rate*.

The flow budget constraint for the representative individual satisfies

$$\dot{w}_t = y - c_t + (s_t - \pi_t)b_t + (i_t - \pi_t)x_t - m_t\pi_t + \text{lump–sum taxes and subsidies}, \tag{3}$$

where y is the constant flow of endowment income in terms of output, and π stands for the instantaneous (actual and expected) rate of inflation. Lump-sum taxes and subsidies are set so as to balance the government budget at every point in time. Let $r = i - \pi = $ real rate of interest. Thus adding and subtracting rw in the right-hand side of equation (3) obtains

$$\dot{w}_t = y + r_t w_t - c_t - (i_t - s_t)b_t - i_t m_t. \tag{4}$$

Ruling out Ponzi games, this differential equation can be integrated to yield the following intertemporal budget constraint:

$$w_0 + \int_0^\infty [y - c_t - (i_t - s_t)b_t - i_t m_t]R_t dt, \tag{5}$$

where $R_t = e^{-\int_0^t r_s ds}$. This is a familiar expression. In standard monetary models, b is devoid of liquidity; thus in equilibrium $s = i$, and the term involving b drops out. However, liquidity services imply that in equilibrium $s < i$.

The representative individual is assumed to maximize utility (1) subject to his intertemporal budget constraint (5) with respect to the paths of c, b, and m, and to take initial wealth w_0 and the paths of i, s, and R as given. This utility maximization is fully conventional except, once again, for the fact that b is assumed to yield liquidity services and thus competes with standard monetary balances, m. At an interior solution (which I assume), the following first-order conditions hold:

$$u'(c_t)e^{-\rho t} = \lambda R_t, \tag{6a}$$

$$v'(m_t)e^{-\rho t} = \lambda R_t i_t, \tag{6b}$$

$$h'(b_t)e^{-\rho t} = \lambda R_t(i_t - s_t), \tag{6c}$$

where λ is the time-invariant (along an equilibrium path) Lagrange multiplier.

I define *total liquidity* (in nominal terms) $Z_t = M_t + B_t$, where M and B are the nominal stocks of conventional money and liquidity-yielding bonds. The monetary/fiscal authority sets the policy interest rate s and total liquidity Z. As will become clear, at equilibrium the composition between M and B is determined by the representative individual. I will focus on rules linking the policy interest rate s with the rate of inflation.

At equilibrium $c_t = y$ for all t. Therefore, by equation (6a), we have that the real interest $r_t = \rho$ for all t. This is a major simplification that allows us to focus entirely on the "liquidity" equations (6b) and (6c). By definition,

M=Pm,   (7a)

B=Pb,   (7b)

where P stands for the nominal price of output (the price level). Hence equilibrium in the liquidity market calls for

$(m_t + b_t)P_t = Z_t.$ (8)

Solving for m and b in equations (6b) and (6c), and recalling that equilibrium $R_t e^{\rho t} = 1$, it can be shown that there are functions Φ and Ψ, such that

$m = \Phi(i) = \Phi(\rho + \pi), \Phi'(\cdot) < 0,$ (9a)

$b = \Omega(i - s) = \Omega(\rho + \pi - s), \Omega'(\cdot) < 0.$ (9b)

Consider an interest rate rule such that

$s = \theta\pi,$ (10)

where θ is a parameter.[7] By equations (8), (9a, 9b), and (10), and assuming, without loss of generality, that the monetary/fiscal authority keeps total liquidity constant at level $\bar{Z}$, it follows that

$$\Phi(\rho + \pi_t) + \Omega(\rho + (1 - \theta)\pi_t) = \frac{\bar{Z}}{P_t}.$$ (11)

Equation (11) implicitly defines a differential equation in P. In (9a) and the first term on the left-hand side of equation (11), π would be an increasing function of P, and hence the system would be unstable around the steady state. Therefore the only converging path is the steady state, and equilibrium would be unique (in a local sense). The second term involving Ω is more problematic. If $\theta \leq 1$, then the implicit differential equation is still unstable around steady state. However, this situation may change if Taylor principle holds, that is,

$\theta > 1$. Consider the limit case in which the demand for conventional money m is totally interest inelastic (e.g., cash in advance), implying $\Phi'=0$ in expression (9b). Therefore, setting $\theta > 1$ implies that the differential equation is stable around steady state, and this ensures the existence of a *continuum* of equilibrium solutions: monetary policy fails to anchor the price level, and sunspot equilibria are possible![8]

Staggered Prices

Here I employ the same model as in the previous section but assume price stickiness as in Calvo (1983). Equations (1) to (6) above hold intact. However, in the present case, output y is demand-determined and, as a rule, will vary over time. Thus, except at steady state, $R_t e^{\delta t} \neq 1$, and R_t is no longer constant over time.

A key step in the derivation will be to express equilibrium m in terms of real total liquidity, that is, $z = Z/P$, equilibrium c and the policy interest rate s. By equations (6a), (6b), and (6c), and also by equation (8), in which $b = z—m$, it follows that

$$h'(z-m)-v'(m)=-u''(c)s. \tag{12}$$

Since the utility indexes are strictly concave and continuously differentiable, there is a function Λ such that at equilibrium

$$m = \Lambda(z,u''(c)s) \quad \text{such that } \Lambda_1 > 0 \text{ and } \Lambda_2 < 0, \tag{13}$$

where $\Lambda_i, i=1,2$ is the partial derivative of Λ with respect to the ith argument.

Log differentiating equation (6a) with respect to time, and using equations (6b), (10), and (13), obtains

$$\dot{c}_t = -\frac{u'(c_t)}{u''(c_t)}\left[\frac{v'(\Lambda(z_t, u'(c_t)\theta\pi_t))}{u'(c_t)} - \rho - \pi_t\right]. \tag{14}$$

Notice that equation (14) is the same as equation (15) in Calvo (1983), except that I have replaced m by function Λ from expression (13); moreover I have employed the policy interest rate s rule (10). These are the only major changes in regard to Calvo (1983). As in Calvo (1983), inflation satisfies

$$\dot{\pi}_t = \beta(\bar{y} - c_t), \beta > 0, \tag{15}$$

where $\bar{y}$ stands for full–employment output.

Finally, recalling that $z = Z/P$, and assuming that Z is held constant over time,[9] we obtain

$$\dot{z}_t = -\pi_t z_t. \tag{16}$$

Linearly approximating system (14)–(16) at steady state (where $\pi = 0$), we get the following expression:

$$A = \begin{pmatrix} \partial\dot{c}/\partial c & \partial\dot{c}/\partial z & \partial\dot{c}/\partial\pi \\ \partial\dot{z}/\partial c & \partial\dot{z}/\partial z & \partial\dot{z}/\partial\pi \\ \partial\dot{\pi}/\partial c & \partial\dot{\pi}/\partial z & \partial\dot{\pi}/\partial\pi \end{pmatrix} = \begin{pmatrix} \rho & -\frac{v''}{u''}\Lambda_1 & \frac{u'}{u''}(1-v''\Lambda_2\theta) \\ 0 & 0 & -\bar{z} \\ -\beta & 0 & 0 \end{pmatrix}, \tag{17}$$

where $\bar{Z}$ denotes real total liquidity at steady state, and time subscripts and arguments are dropped to simplify the notation.

Let γ_i, $i = 1, 2, 3$, be the characteristic roots of matrix A. Then, as is well known (see Gantmacher 1956), and recalling that $\Lambda_1 > 0$,

$$\gamma_1\gamma_2\gamma_3 = DetA = -\frac{v''}{u''}\Lambda_1\beta\bar{z} < 0, \tag{18a}$$

$$\gamma_1 + \gamma_2 + \gamma_3 = TraceA = \rho > 0. \tag{18b}$$

Therefore, by (18a, 18b), system (17) displays one negative root and two roots with positive real parts, which ensures local existence and uniqueness of a converging equilibrium path (given that z is the only predetermined variable). Notice that this result holds *independently* of parameter θ, since it does not show up in steady-state conditions (18a, 18b).[10] This implies that, contrary to a model in which b yields no liquidity services, monetary rule (10) ensures a nominal anchor even though it does not satisfy Taylor' principle.

Closing Remarks

Recent financial crises have shown the importance of liquidity and liquidity shocks, issues that central banks tend to ignore under normal circumstances. This chapter suggests that if assets whose interest rates are tightly linked to policy interest rates (e.g., short-term Treasury bills) are also means of exchange or employed as collaterals, the conditions under which monetary policy provides a nominal anchor may differ from those in models in which those assets are starkly different from high-powered money—as is the case in the dominant monetary paradigm prior to the subprime crisis. This holds true despite the fact that the model involves a small addition to the barebones central bank model discussed in the chapter 3.

Is liquidity an important topic for crisis times only, or should it also be modeled under normal circumstances? In my view, most major financial innovations are attempts to imbue liquidity into otherwise illiquid assets. As argued in Calvo (2012b) and previous chapters, this has the potential of, for instance, stemming a real estate bubble associated with the creation of mortgage-backed securities. This can be shown to hold under rational expectations. It is thus unlikely that monetary policy, one of whose key roles is inflation targeting, will be immune to these developments. It is unlikely that we will be able to separate money from other assets; as argued in this book, creation of liquidity by the private sector may be affected by monetary and regulatory policy, including the expectation of bailouts if liquid assets are subject to runs. Therefore central banks should be encouraged to bring liquidity into their radar, especially in their inflation targeting models. In doing so, incidentally, it will quickly become apparent that *total liquidity*, including monetary aggregates, will recover the prominent role it plays in quantity theory models. This is illustrated by the models above in which *total liquidity*, Z, is not endogenous even though the central controls the liquid-bond interest rate. If total liquidity was endogenous and left free to be determined by market forces, inflation will not be anchored in interior solutions, no matter how large one sets policy coefficient θ, which stands in sharp contrast with the dominant monetary theory paradigm.[11] This does not imply, of course, that interest rate rules are not worth exploring. But it comes a distant second to liquidity management, especially in staggered-price frameworks in which, as suggested by the results in this chapter, interest rules would play a secondary role in inflation anchoring.

5 Liquidity Crunch/Trap: Some Unconventional Output/Employment/ Growth Implications[1]

Through banking, he who possesses wealth difficult to exchange can create a circulating medium. He has only to give to a bank his note – for which, of course, his property is liable – get in return the right to draw, and lo! his comparatively unexchangeable wealth becomes liquid currency.

Irving Fisher (1912, p. 41).

Introduction

As I pointed out in chapters 2, the liquidity approach is strongly motivated by a phenomenon that has played a key role in the subprime crisis, namely the sudden value loss of financial assets employed as collateral, especially by shadow banks (e.g., see Gorton and Metrick 2012). The reasons behind this devaluation are varied, going from corruption to fundamental economic factors. I do not dwell on the micro-foundations of a sudden loss of value, which I have being calling liquidity crunch in this book. Instead, in most of the chapter, I discuss the *mechanics* following a liquidity crunch under the assumption that there are some liquid bonds utilized by firms as collateral or, more generally, *media of exchange* that can be subject to liquidity crunch (e.g., a run on repos). I will assume that firms can utilize private sector bonds (e.g., asset-backed securities) or money (called "cash") that could be associated with public sector liquid liabilities (high-powered money, Treasury bills, etc.) for these purposes. Thus a liquidity crunch on private sector bonds tends to lower the supply of liquid bonds in terms of output, and eventually drive firms to hold cash in their liquid portfolio, even though under normal circumstances cash is dominated by bonds. As a result a liquidity crunch on bonds can increase the demand for cash by firms and give rise to *price deflation*—the scourge of the 1930s Great Depression, and a phenomenon that central banks in developed markets (DM) saw as serious threat during the Lehman crisis.

The reader should be warned that *realism* is not a central objective in this chapter. Rather, *simplicity* is a guiding principle because when reality is as complex as in the present instance, realism could be self-defeating—and Occam's razor is in order. Thus, in contrast to much of the financial crisis literature (e.g., see Gertler and Karadi 2011; Gertler and Kiyotaki 2010, 2014), I do not include banks or credit in the model. The model is a simple extension of the conventional cash-in-advance literature where the main additions are

• private sector bonds are brought to bear as liquid assets instead of only cash, and
• firms are subject to a liquidity-in-advance constraint where liquid bonds play a key role.

This is enough to generate some *realistic mechanics*, including phenomena akin to credit Sudden Stop (despite the model's simplicity). For example, a liquidity crunch on private sector bonds gives rise to a phenomenon akin to the liquidity trap, that is, a sudden increase in the demand for cash that does not rely on the more familiar assumption that the appetite for cash is prompted by a sudden realization that investment opportunities have lost their shine. I do not discuss why cash keeps its shine while bond prices melt down, but I do discuss this important phenomenon elsewhere under Price Theory of Money (see Calvo 2012a, 2013a, and chapter 2 in this book). In a nutshell, cash is more resilient than liquid bonds because many prices and wages are set in terms of cash in a staggered fashion (although, again, for the sake of simplicity, in the present model prices are assumed to be perfectly flexible). Incidentally, I will discuss a closed-economy model with only one type of cash, thus ignoring the challenging issues related to the existence of multiple currencies. This, coupled with the assumed resilience of cash as a liquid asset, makes the approach better suited to address issues raised by the subprime crisis in DM, especially the United States.

The basic model lays bare phenomena that are likely to hold true in more complex and perhaps more realistic models, in which liquidity crunch has supply effects. Models in which money enters production functions may have opposite effects to the ones found in standard models in which liquidity is an argument in utility functions (recall chapter 3). The same holds true in the present model, where a more general concept, namely "liquidity," enters indirectly as a factor of production. I will show, for instance, that lowering the central bank policy or reference interest rate, and increasing the rate of inflation are contractionary.

To be sure, the view that money demand is associated with production or investment is not new. As pointed out in chapter 3, it harks back at least to Keynes's "Finance Motive" for holding money, an issue that was ignored in the *General Theory* but that Keynes later recognized as important (e.g., see Davidson 1965; Tsiang 1980). One simple version of the Finance Motive is closely linked to the assumption that investment is subject to a cash-in-advance constraint, an assumption that was much later studied in Stockman (1981).[2] In the present chapter a similar constraint will be assumed with "liquidity" substituted for "cash"—a constraint that applies to output in the static model and investment in the dynamic extension. An appendix shows that the models can be couched in terms of a conventional representative-consumer general equilibrium setup.

Basic Model

Consider an economy with two types of media of exchange, denoted M and B. M can be interpreted as high-powered money plus highly liquid public debt instruments like Treasury bills, and will be called "cash"; B is also a medium of exchange (e.g., it circulates) but is more akin to a *liquid* bond. The reader may want to think of B as asset-backed securities, although I will model it as a simple consol. Output, y, is homogeneous and can be used for consumption, c, or as raw material, x. The production function is $f(x)$, where f satisfies standard regularity conditions.[3] For simplicity, I assume that there are no production lags.[4]

This is a world of representative-consumers and firms. Firms and consumers are atomistic and their number is equal to 1. Thus there is no need to use different notation for individual and aggregate decisions. Consumers are subject to the standard cash-in-advance constraint, which I will express as follows:

$$M^H = Pc, \tag{1}$$

where M^H is cash held by households, and P is the price of output in terms of cash. Since output is putty-putty that can be costlessly allocated either to consumption or raw materials, in the interior solutions (assumed here) the nominal price of consumption and raw materials is P.

Firms are also subject to a similar constraint—which could be called "liquidity-in-advance"—but firms are free either to use cash or B. The constraint takes the following form:

$$M^F + \theta SB = Px, \tag{2}$$

where M^F is cash held by firms, S is the price of B in terms of cash, or *nominal* price of B. Parameter θ $(0 \leq \theta < 1)$ is a measure of B's effectiveness as a medium of exchange; $1 - \theta$ is akin to the haircut on repo bonds (e.g., see Gorton and Metrick 2012): as the haircut increases, $1 - \theta$ would go up. Equation (2) captures a situation in which, through repos and other financial devices, firms are able to pay for raw materials, x, by means other than cash. An alternative interpretation of the role of B—more in line with standard practice—is that these bonds are employed as collateral for trade credit associated with the purchase of raw materials, x. However, their effectiveness can be subject to shocks, as is the case with all liquid assets that are not protected by a lender of last resort.[5] Moreover instruments like B are assumed to be inconvenient media of exchange for regular consumers. This twist in the standard model helps capture some salient phenomena in the subprime and related crises that have been largely ignored in the outstanding literature.[6]

I focus on steady-state solutions, and assume that there is a "pure" bond that cannot be employed as a medium of exchange and yields an output rate of return equal to r. I identify r with the *real* interest rate, and let π denote the one-period-ahead expected rate of inflation (or the right-hand derivative of the log of expected P in continuous time). Hence we can abstract from random shocks so that in continuous time the nominal interest rate i on non-liquid bonds satisfies

$$i = r + \pi. \tag{3}$$

Let i^B denote the nominal interest rate on B.[7] Consider the problem faced by a profit-maximizing firm that plans on utilizing raw materials in an amount equal to x. Recall equation (2), so here the nominal opportunity cost associated with this decision is equal to

$$iM^F + (i - i^B)SB = i(Px - \theta SB) + (i - i^B)SB, \tag{4}$$

where i^B is the (implicit) nominal rate of return on B (to be further discussed below). Hence minimization of the right-hand side expression in (4), implies that

$$i > \frac{i - i^B}{\theta} \Rightarrow M^F = 0. \tag{5}$$

In other words, if the inequality in expression (5) holds, it is optimal for the firm to hold its entire liquid assets in the form of liquid bonds, B. The opposite holds, meaning $B = 0$, if the inequality goes in the opposite direction. I will later assume that the supply of B is given, which implies that i^B will be accommodated in equilibrium to ensure that B's demand and supply are equated. Hence, if the supply of $B > 0$, this will rule out the case in which $\theta i < i - i^B$, namely the inequality opposite to the one displayed in expression (5).

Let Z be the nominal coupon on B which, to make it consistent with steady state, I will assume grows at the rate of inflation π, constant over time. Hence, at a steady state where S also grows at rate π, we have

$$i^B = \frac{Z}{S} + \pi = constant. \tag{6}$$

I will now start the discussion by examining the case in which the firm chooses to hold its entire liquid portfolio in the form of bonds, B, so that inequality (5) holds. Nominal profit equals

$$f(x)P - xP - (i - i^B)SB. \tag{7}$$

Hence, denoting the relative price of B in terms of output by $s = S/P$, and the output value of the coupon by $z = Z/P$—and recalling equations (3) and (6)—I can now express profits in terms of output as

$$f(x) - x - (i - i^B)sB = f(x) - x - \left(r - \frac{z}{s}\right)sB =$$
$$f(x) - \left[1 + \frac{1}{\theta}\left(r - \frac{z}{s}\right)\right]x, \tag{8}$$

where the expression on the right-hand side employs liquidity constraint (2), since $M^F = 0$ implies that $\theta sB = x$. Hence, the first-order condition with respect to x is

$$f'(x) = 1 + \frac{1}{\theta}\left(r - \frac{z}{s}\right). \tag{9}$$

At equilibrium, the liquidity-in-advance condition holds, that is, $\theta s\bar{B} = x$, where $\bar{B}$ denotes the constant supply of liquid bonds. Thus, taking the latter and equation (9) into account, at equilibrium, we have

$$f'(x) + \frac{z\bar{B}}{x} = 1 + \frac{r}{\theta}. \tag{10}$$

Hence, recalling that, by strict concavity, $f'' < 0$, we can prove that in the region in which only liquid bonds are held in firms' portfolios, at equilibrium,

$$\frac{dx}{d\theta} > 0. \tag{11}$$

I will define a liquidity crunch as a fall in parameter θ. Therefore expression (11) states that a liquidity crunch results in output contraction. This is a perfectly intuitive result, given that, *ceteris paribus*, a fall in θ increases the opportunity cost of the firms' liquidity constraint. However, this result is still not enough to generate pressures for price deflation. Let $\bar{M}$ denote cash supply, which for much of the rest of this chapter is exogenous and, at steady state, grows at the rate of inflation. Then, recalling that firms do not hold cash and equation (1), we have

$$P = \frac{\bar{M}}{c}. \tag{12}$$

Moreover, since output is putty-putty that can be costlessly allocated to consumption or raw materials, we have

$$f(x) = x + c. \tag{13}$$

Thus, by equations (12) and (13),

$$P = \frac{\bar{M}}{f(x) - x}. \tag{14}$$

Henceforth, I will focus on the "normal" case in which the nominal rate of return on pure bonds that do not yield liquidity services, denoted here by i exceeds i^B. This implies, by (6) and (9), that

$$f'(x) - 1 > 0, \tag{15}$$

from which it follows that consumption increases with output and moreover, by (11), (14), and (15),

$$\frac{dP}{d\theta} < 0. \tag{16}$$

Hence, a liquidity crunch caused by a contraction in the liquidity parameter θ is associated with a price *rise*, not deflation!

The situation may change if the fall in θ induces firms to hold cash. This is an interesting case. Recalling the discussion around equation (5), this can hold in equilibrium only if firms are indifferent between cash and bonds. For that to be the case, we must have

$$i = \frac{i - i^B}{\theta}. \tag{17}$$

Therefore profits in terms of output take the following functional form (cf. equation 8):

$$f(x) - (1 + i)x, \tag{18}$$

and the profit-maximizing value of x, denoted by x^*, is independent of θ, and the first-order condition satisfies:

$$f'(x^*) = 1 + i. \tag{19}$$

From (6), (9), and (19), it can easily be verified that solutions in which firms hold their entire liquid portfolio in the form of liquid bonds, imply $x \geq x^*$. In other words, liquid bonds that dominate cash return-wise are conducive to higher productivity.

Before proceeding, I will establish that there is a critical value of $\theta = \theta^*$, such that if $\theta < \theta^*$, firms will start holding cash and, thus, output will be equal to $f(x^*)$. By equation (9) and liquidity constraint that applies when no cash is held by firms, meaning $\theta s \bar{B} = x$, we get

$$f'(x) = 1 + \frac{1}{\theta}(i - i^B) = 1 + \frac{1}{\theta}\left(r - \frac{z}{s}\right) = 1 + \frac{r}{\theta} - \frac{z\bar{B}}{x}. \tag{20}$$

Previous results have shown that x declines as θ falls (recall expression (11)). Hence the fourth expression in (20) rises as θ falls, or equivalently,

$$\frac{1}{\theta}\left(i - i^B\right) \quad \text{rises as } \theta \text{ falls,}$$

and it moves toward i. It actually hits i if equilibrium $x = x^*$. Suppose that even though x falls as θ goes down, it never hits x^*. This is a contradiction because in that case there would exist some x, $\underline{x} > 0$, such that $\underline{x} \leq$ equilibrium x, for all θ. Under these conditions, the right-most expression in (20) converges to $+\infty$, while $f'(x) \leq f'(\underline{x})$, contradicting equality condition in expression (20). Therefore there exists a θ^* such that $i = \left(i - i^B\right)/\theta^*$, and $x = x^*$, as asserted. For any $\theta < \theta^*$, the corresponding equilibrium $x = x^*$. Summarizing, these results show that assuming that at the initial liquidity coefficient θ firms hold no cash and instead hold their entire liquid portfolio in bonds, a decline in θ increases the opportunity cost of liquidity and leads to output contraction. Eventually, as θ keeps falling, bonds become equally costly than cash. Further θ contraction beyond that point has no effect on output, and the opportunity cost of holding liquidity is constant at i.

However, that does not imply that bonds will be absent from firms' portfolios. The model assumes that individuals will never find it advantageous to hold B. Hence, in equilibrium, firms must end up being the ultimate holders of $\bar{B}$. What happens is that in order for B to be an attractive liquid investment for firms, its return has to compensate for the smallness of θ, a situation that requires such a large fall in the output price of B, denoted by s, that the supply of bonds would not be enough to satisfy firms' demand for liquid assets (i.e., firms' liquidity-in-advance constraint). More formally, in the region where firms have a positive demand for cash, bonds must have the same opportunity cost as cash. Thus, recalling equation (7), we have

$$i = \frac{i - i^B}{\theta},$$

implying, by equation (6), that

$$i^B = \frac{z}{s} + \pi = (1 - \theta)i = (1 - \theta)(r + \pi).$$

Hence

$$s = \frac{z}{(1 - \theta)r - \theta\pi}, \qquad (21)$$

from which it follows that, as expected, the output price of the liquid bond falls as its liquidity θ contracts. Notice, incidentally, that in this region the supply of bonds, $\bar{B}$, has no effect on their output price, s.

By equation (21), liquidity services of the liquid bond satisfy

$$s\theta\bar{B} = \frac{\theta z\bar{B}}{(1 - \theta)r - \theta\pi}, \qquad (22)$$

which falls as B suffers liquidity crunch (or $\bar{B}$ falls, a result that will come in handy in the next section). Since, as pointed out above, in this region output is constant and there is a positive demand for cash, we have, by equations (2) and (22),

$$\frac{M^F}{P} + \theta s\bar{B} = \frac{M^F}{P} + \frac{\theta z\bar{B}}{(1 - \theta)r - \theta\pi} = x^*. \qquad (23)$$

Hence

$$M^F = \left[x^* - \frac{\theta z \bar{B}}{(1-\theta)r - \theta\pi} \right] P, \tag{24}$$

implying that, given the price level P, firms' demand for cash *rise* as liquid bonds become less liquid, a basic factor behind price deflationary pressures discussed below.

Consider now the demand for cash by households. In this region, output and the input of raw materials are constant and unresponsive to changes in θ. Thus

$$Pc = P[f(x^*) - x^*] = M^H. \tag{25}$$

Equilibrium in the cash market calls for

$$\bar{M} = M^H + M^F = \left[-\frac{\theta z \bar{B}}{(1-\theta)r - \theta\pi} + f(x^*) \right] P, \tag{26}$$

where the right-most expression comes from equations (24) and (25). Consequently a liquidity crunch on B increases the demand for cash and causes a fall in the price level, that is, deflation. This is a central result of this chapter. For future reference, I will call the region in which firms hold cash in their liquid portfolio the liquidity trap region.

These results are intuitive and highly relevant. Suppose that firms start at a situation in which they hold their entire portfolio in the form of liquid bonds, B. A slight loss of liquidity has a negative impact on output but the price level rises. This is akin to *stagflation*. However, if the liquidity crunch takes up major proportions, output will fall more, of course, together with the price of liquid assets—but the price level may fall. This is because firms' demand for cash rises and brings about a fall in the price level. Interestingly, the central bank can prevent price deflation by increasing cash supply, something that DM central banks carried out during the subprime crisis. But, even though a once-and-for-all increase in the supply of cash may help prevent price deflation, it does not change the opportunity cost of liquidity, implying that it will have no effect on output and, by (21), bond relative prices. This straightforward result shows that *liquidity crunch on private-created liquidity may have a negative output effects that may not be offset by an equivalent increase in public sector liquidity* ("money"). This puts into question the Friedman–Schwartz (1963) conjecture that the US Great Depression could have been avoided if the Fed increased money supply in order to avert price deflation. The relevance of the result here is enhanced by the fact that lack of price deflation in the United States was not enough to prevent large output loss.[8]

Extension: Endogenous Bond Return, z

I now show that the initial shock associated with liquidity crunch can be amplified by subsequent effects on the rate of return on liquid bonds, caused by liquidity crunch. I will assume that the "missing" factor in $f(x)$ is "land." Land is in fixed supply and its quantity is normalized to 1. I will now assume that $\bar{B}$ is a claim on the return of a unit of land. Hence

$$z\bar{B} = f(x) - f'(x)x, \quad \frac{d(z\bar{B})}{dx} = -f''(x)x > 0. \tag{27}$$

For the sake of brevity, I will focus on the non–liquidity trap region where firms' liquid portfolio is entirely composed of liquid bonds B. Hence, by equations (10) and (27), it follows that a liquidity crunch has a larger negative effect on output than in the case in which z is constant. Moreover

$$\frac{f(x)}{x} = 1 + \frac{r}{\theta}. \qquad (28)$$

For simplicity, let us assume that $f(x) = x^{\alpha}, 0 < \alpha < 1$. This implies, by equation (28), that

$$\ln x = -\frac{1}{1-\alpha} \ln\left(1 + \frac{r}{\theta}\right).$$

Therefore the impact of a change in θ on x converges to ∞ (in absolute value) as α goes to 1.

This extension illustrates in a straightforward manner how a liquidity crunch can end up having severe real effects that go far beyond the initial shock.

Parallels with Sudden Stop

Firms' liquidity constraint and liquidity crunch can mimic, to some extent, the mechanics and implications of credit sudden stop (see the definition in chapters 6 and 7). In the present chapter, destruction of firms' liquidity amounts to a negative supply shock. When credit is explicitly modeled and assumed to be constrained by collateral (as in the seminal paper by Kiyotaki and Moore 1997), liquidity crunch lowers collateral values, giving rise to credit Sudden Stop, which in turn hinders output and/or growth. The details are different but the reduced forms are uncannily similar. The advantage of the present approach is that it shows that liquidity crunch—which some people believe can be easily remedied through expansionary monetary policy—can block the credit channel and have severe effects on the real economy.

Monetary Policy and Growth

Monetary Policy

A common advice for getting out of a liquidity trap is making cash less attractive by increasing the rate of inflation, π (e.g., see Krugman 2012). Presumably, higher inflation lowers the demand for money and increases aggregate demand. Under a New Keynesian model with sticky prices, higher aggregate demand translates into higher output. However, in the present setup in which prices are perfectly flexible, higher inflation carries opposite effects. This has been discussed in Chapter 3 under the assumption that firms hold cash. Consider now the case in which firms hold no cash. Equation (10) shows that the opportunity cost of firms' liquidity holdings is not affected by π, implying that output will remain the same as π rises. However, by equation (19), x^* falls, which shrinks the liquidity trap region. None of this has a significant effect on the real sector because prices are flexible. However, shrinking the liquidity trap region would be welcome if price inflexibility becomes an issue, a realistic outcome if the equilibrium price-level contraction is large.

Many central banks, especially in DM, use a policy or reference interest rate to conduct monetary policy. If such interest rate is identified with i in the model, it is straightforward to show that lowering the policy interest rate is expansionary. However, this will be hard to justify in the present model because, under those circumstances, Fisherian equation (3) need not apply. An alternative is to think of M, called cash in the text, as a combination of cash properly speaking and, say, highly liquid Treasury Bills. This is the approach taken in chapter 4, and in Calvo (2012b), which follows on the footsteps of a number of papers co-authored with Carlos

Végh (e.g., 1995). A shortcut is to assume that the central bank pays interest on cash, i_M, and to identify the latter with the central bank policy interest rate. It is easy to see that the opportunity cost of holding cash is $i - i_M$, and that lowering i_M brings about results opposite to the conventional ones: It *depresses* output in the region in which firms hold cash, while the effect on output is nil otherwise. Moreover quantitative easing (QE) that increases the stock of cash in exchange for public debt (called "operation twist") would have negligible effects in the context of the Calvo–Végh type model because it simply does not change M (i.e., the aggregate of cash and public debt).

The situation is different if QE takes the form of central bank's purchases of "toxic assets" that in the present context can be modeled as a purchase of B in exchange for M, assuming, as customary in monetary theory, that the return on B (i.e., z) is rebated to consumers as lump-sum transfers. This is tantamount to engineering a fall in the stock of B held by firms (i.e., $\bar{B}$ in our notation) coupled with an increase in cash supply (i.e., $\bar{M}$). It is easy to verify, by expression (26), that in the liquidity trap region this policy has no impact on output but it increases excess supply of cash, leading to a rise in the price level P. This could be welcome if a price fall is socially costly (e.g., Fisher's 1933, *Debt Deflation*).[9] Consider now the case outside the liquidity trap region in which firms hold their liquid portfolio entirely in the form of B. By equation (10), a fall in $\bar{B}$ is associated with output *contraction*. To help intuition, recall that, by equation (2), outside the liquidity trap region, liquidity constraint boils down to $\theta s \bar{B} = x$. Suppose that, contradicting the preceding statement, the fall in $\bar{B}$ is accompanied by a rise in x. Thus the liquidity constraint and equation (6) imply that s rises and i^B falls. The latter increases liquidity's opportunity cost and leads to a fall in intermediate goods, x, and output—a contradiction. It should be noted, though, that the assumption that θ is constant may be too strong. For example, if by means of QE the central bank sends a signal that it will operate as a lender of last resort with respect to B, QE could actually restore full liquidity to toxic assets and prevent liquidity crunch. However, this was not the message sent by DM central banks after the 2008 Lehman episode: haircuts on some important repo assets remained high relative to pre-crisis levels (see Gorton and Metrick 2012). Thus the more nuanced lesson is that unless QE succeeds in raising the liquidity of toxic assets to offset the decline in the supply of toxic bonds, QE could be counterproductive.[10]

It is worth pointing out, however, that if the public debt (which can easily be appended to the above model) enjoys high liquidity (i.e., high θ) and offers a rate of return equivalent to that displayed by B prior to liquidity crunch, a government purchase of B in exchange for public debt is capable of offsetting the effects of the liquidity crunch on B. Actually the beneficial effects of a larger stock of public debt would hold even if it stems from fiscal deficit, unless the latter has a detrimental effect on public debt's liquidity.[11] This issue, incidentally, deserves closer scrutiny. Keynesian economists tend to look approvingly at fiscal deficit to the extent that it is associated with larger government expenditure. The analysis here suggests that even if aggregate demand is not directly stimulated by government, fiscal deficits may have positive supply effects by increasing the stock of liquid assets. It is worth saying, though, that the effectiveness of this policy depends on the strength of the output anchor of the currency in terms of which the public bond is denominated and the belief that the government would fully back up those bonds with such a currency. Hence the positive effect of fiscal deficit is more likely to happen in reserve-currency economies such as the US and the EU currencies than in EMs.

These results show that if bonds play a central role in firms' payment system, there are instances in which conventional policy results do not hold. Such policies may be totally ineffective and, in some cases, outcomes may be diametrically opposed to the conventional ones. For example, lower policy interest rates and QE purchases of toxic assets may depress output in the non–liquidity trap region, unless QE has a sufficiently large impact on the liquidity of those assets.

Growth

The model can be easily extended to a growth context by assuming an A-K technology, cost of adjustment for investment and a liquidity-in-advance constraint for firms like in equation (2). In what follows I will sketch out the model, leaving the straightforward details to the interested reader.

I write the production function as AK, where K is the capital stock, technical parameter $A > 1 + \tau$, and τ is the opportunity cost of liquidity. Let ι denote the ratio of investment to capital. Hence

$$\frac{\dot{K}_t}{K_t} = \iota_t - \delta, \tag{29}$$

where δ is the constant nonnegative rate of depreciation. Let the cost of adjustment be given by $\psi(\iota)K$, where function ψ is increasing, twice-continuously differentiable, and strictly convex. Liquidity-in-advance equals gross investment $= \iota K$. Therefore, for given time-invariant real rate of interest rate r, and opportunity cost of liquidity, the present-discounted value of the firm at t_0 is given by

$$\int_{t_0}^{\infty} \{A - [1 + \tau \iota_t + \psi(\iota_t)]\} K_t e^{-r(t-t_0)} dt,$$

which, taking equation (29) into account, boils down to

$$K_{t_0} \int_{t_0}^{\infty} \{A - [1 + \tau \iota_t + \psi(\iota_t)]\} e^{-\int_{t_0}^t (r + \delta - \iota_v) dv} dt. \tag{30}$$

The firm's optimization problem consists in maximizing expression (30) by choosing the path of ι from t_0 to infinity, taking the initial capital stock as given. A brief perusal of expression (30) reveals that the optimum ι-path is independent of K_{t_0}. Moreover the firm faces the same problem at any future time. Hence optimal ι is constant over time, and expression (30) boils down to

$$\frac{A - [1 + \tau \iota + \psi(\iota)]}{r + \delta - \iota} \equiv J(\iota). \tag{31}$$

The firm's value maximization problem consists in maximizing expression (31) with respect to ι. At an interior optimum $J' = 0$. More explicitly,

$$J'(\iota) = \frac{-[\tau + \psi'(\iota)](r + \delta - \iota) + A - 1 - \tau \iota - \psi(\iota)}{(r + \delta - \iota)^2} = 0. \tag{32}$$

It can be easily verified that at a point where first-order condition (31) holds, the second-order condition $J''(\iota) < 0$ also holds. Moreover, by (32) and the fact that at an interior optimum $r + \delta - \iota > 0$,

$$\frac{\partial J'(\iota)}{\partial \tau} < 0,$$

which implies that

$$\frac{\partial \iota}{\partial \tau} < 0. \tag{33}$$

This shows, recalling equation (29), that the economy's growth rate is a decreasing function of the opportunity cost of liquidity. Thus, assuming that r is invariant to changes in the growth rate, we are now in the position of translating all the central results of previous section to a growth context. For example, on impact, a liquidity crunch (i.e., a fall in θ) has no effect on output but lowers the growth rate. It is worth noting, however, that instant effects can easily be recovered if the model is expanded by assuming that output requires raw material.

The appendix presents a general equilibrium version of the models in this chapter, and it shows that in a closed economy and in a growth context the real rate of interest r moves in the same direction as the growth rate ι. By equation (32), we have

$$\frac{\partial J'(\iota)}{\partial r} < 0,$$

where the derivative is evaluated at $J'(\iota) = 0$. Hence

$$\frac{\partial \iota}{\partial r} < 0. \tag{34}$$

This shows that a lower r associated with a rise in the opportunity cost of liquidity, τ, cushions the latter's impact on growth. However, it also lowers the return on bonds associated with firm's profits, which has an opposite effect. Clearly, a fuller analysis calls for more explicit modeling of the production and adjustment cost functions.[12]

Slow Jobless/Wageless Recovery after Crisis: Key Items for the Research Agenda

The models in this chapter can be applied to rationalize two highly topical phenomena: slow growth (and possibly secular recession) and jobless recovery after financial crisis triggered by liquidity crunch—including high-inflation cases in which there is no jobless recovery but real wages are much lower at the output recovery point than their levels prior to crisis. A first approximation to these issues is sketched out below.

Slow Growth

Reinhart and Reinhart (2010), among others, offer compelling evidence that recovery after financial crisis is significantly slower than in standard recessions. The subprime crisis confirms this view, and the growth model in the preceding section offers a dynamic framework in which the Reinhart–Reinhart results are rationalized if liquidity crunch is a persistent phenomenon. The missing piece, of course, is persistence of a low θ. However, the task may be simpler than it looks, because in a more realistic model with shadow banks and credit, a liquidity crunch directly blocks up the credit channel and, under incomplete financial markets, generates familiar "domino" effects, which help spread the credit crisis beyond the original banks involved in the liquidity crunch episode (e.g., shadow banks). Market incompleteness implies that unfulfilled credit contracts will be registered as being in "default" and subject to bankruptcy procedures, a time-consuming process and, perhaps more important, a nontransparent one that puts into question the reliability of the credit channel for potential lenders—and detracts from the liquidity of the associated assets. The issue is eminently empirical but the advantage of the approach explored in this chapter is that it traces the source of slow growth to liquidity and credit issues that can be measured and tested. Available evidence for emerging markets offers some support for the liquidity/credit conjecture for slow growth, given that output recovers to pre-crisis levels even though credit stays significantly below (see Calvo, Izquierdo, and Talvi 2006, and chapter 6).

Jobless/Wageless Recovery

There is ample evidence that the labor market is severely hit after financial crisis. Calvo, Coricelli, and Ottonello (2012, 2013), and chapter 6, conjecture that part of the reason is that those crises are associated with liquidity crunch and meltdown in collateral output values. As the argument goes, expenditure associated with labor costs (e.g., hiring costs) do not enjoy as much "intrinsic collateral" as those associated with capital investment, for example. This phenomenon might slant the balance against labor and induce the adoption of more capital-intensive techniques. This slows down hiring if wages are downward inflexible, or depress real wages otherwise.

One can illustrate the implications of this phenomenon by a slight modification of the growth model in the preceding section. The production function can be written as follows:

$$Af(x), \tag{35}$$

where x now stands for labor input, and A for TFP. If the real wage is constant and equal to 1, and the opportunity cost of liquidity-in-advance is again denoted by τ, the firm's optimization problem becomes

$$\text{Max}_x[Af(x) - x(1 + \tau)]. \tag{36}$$

The liquidity/collateral constraint is involved in the $x\tau$ term in expression (36), which excludes the missing factor "land" in function f. Hence this corresponds to the extreme case in which the constraint applies only to labor services. Land has its own intrinsic collateral.[13] In parallel with the model in the section above, a rise in the opportunity cost of liquidity τ, pushes down employment and output. As TFP, A, increases over time, output goes up accompanied by employment but, clearly, output recovers to its pre-crisis level prior to employment—and jobless recovery holds.

An alternative exercise is to assume perfect wage flexibility and full employment. I will not discuss the details of this case. However, it is clear that the real wage will fall on impact, but output and employment will remain invariant. This is an instance of what Calvo, Coricelli, and Ottonello (2012) call "wageless" recovery. Notice that even though no output/employment effects occur on impact, long-run growth is bound to decline, following the logic I noted at the start of this chapter.

Appendix

Let us first consider the liquidity model discussed at the beginning of the chapter to see that it is possible to make the real interest rate r endogenous by assuming a representative individual whose utility function satisfies

$$\int_0^\infty u(c_t)e^{-\rho t}dt, \tag{A1}$$

where u is increasing in c, strictly concave and twice-continuously differentiable—and ρ is a positive parameter that stands for the individual's subjective rate of time preference. Therefore it can easily be shown that at steady state in which output is constant through time, $r = \rho$ at equilibrium.[14]

The situation is slightly more complicated in a growth context. Let the instantaneous utility function satisfy

$$u(c) = \frac{c^{1-\beta}}{1-\beta},$$

(A2)

where $\beta > 0$, and if $\beta = 1$, expression (A2) boils down to $u(c) = \ln c$. Hence, recalling that, by equation (29), the growth rate equals $\iota - \delta$, the corresponding Euler equation is

$$\frac{\dot{c}}{c} = \frac{r - \rho}{\beta} = \iota - \delta.$$

(A3)

From which it follows that

$$r = (\iota - \delta)\beta + \rho.$$

(A4)

Hence, as stated in the text, there is a positive association between the real interest rate and the steady-state rate of growth.

II Emerging Market Crises through the Lens of the Liquidity Approach

Introduction to Part II

As noted in chapters 1 and 2, there are strong indications that deep financial crises that have taken place since the mid-1990s cannot be easily explained by standard economic fundamentals. The discussion in those chapters leaned strongly toward conjectures that put liquidity phenomena center stage and, as a first approximation, toward the assumption that liquidity shocks have an important random exogenous component. In the chapters that follow, I let the numbers "speak for themselves" and explore those conjectures in a more systematic manner.

A major roadblock of empirical analysis is to be able to find identifying restrictions that enjoy a wide appeal in the profession. This is hard to achieve for global financial crises as the Great Depression and the Lehman crisis, because these are episodes in which virtually everyone and everything are involved. Fortunately, these problems are less acute if the analysis puts much weight on EMs where the source of the shock is "external" to most of them. This helps attribute the ensuing effects to those shocks. Moreover these chapters will focus on episodes in which the effects are large and largely unanticipated. But it is worth pointing out that by "largely unanticipated," I try to capture low-probability events, for which it is plausible to expect that they will cause severe financial turmoil in individual economies. This makes the analysis more relevant and attuned with the previous discussion in the book, since, as discussed in chapter 1, global crises since the mid-1990s can be claimed to be large and triggered by low-probability shocks.

Large and abrupt reversals in external credit flows will be called Sudden Stops (Calvo 1998). Moreover Sudden Stops that follow on the footsteps of a global financial shock will be labeled Systemic Sudden Stops (or 3S, for short). Given the thrust of this book, and the fact that Systemic Sudden Stops have no clear roots in standard fundamentals and effects are large, it is natural to conjecture that those shocks have central liquidity components, such as liquidity crunch.

The chapters that follow are basically exploratory and take the systemic liquidity shock as given. Chapter 6 (co-authored with Pablo Ottonello) will describe the main features associated with 3S episodes. Chapter 7 will dwell more deeply into the factors that enhance the probability of SS in the context of a systemic crisis. I will now turn to give a more detailed overview of these chapters.

Chapter 6 will characterize 3S crises and show that these episodes are radically different from "regular" recession episodes. A salient characteristic is that there is much less room for consumption smoothing. Thus the shock has to be absorbed in the short run, which tends to exacerbate its social cost in a significant way. Besides, 3S crises last longer than other recessions and have a more deleterious effect on the labor market and investment. Moreover, although 3S have a clear financial cause behind them, reflected in a sharp contraction of international and domestic credit, output rebound is less dependent on those credit sources. In particular, international credit takes much longer than output to recover pre-crisis levels. This suggests that the original credit sources are probably substituted for less efficient ones, which help explain the persistent effects of these episodes (see chapter 5 for a model in which less efficient intermediation has a negative effect on growth). Hence we could conjecture, employing an expression due to Larry Summers, that 3S give rise to *secular stagnation*.

Chapter 7 (co-authored with Alejandro Izquierdo and Luis-Fernando Mejía) makes a stronger effort in identifying the probability of SS, taking global factors as given (and captured by a time dummy in the regressions). Based on a panel of SS episodes in the period 1990 to 2004, the paper shows that in a systemic financial crisis the probability of SS is enhanced by the current account deficit (CAD) and domestic liability dollarization (DLD). The latter is intended to measure currency-denomination mismatch in the domestic capital market. More specifically, DLD is an estimate of foreign exchange denominated loans by domestic banks as a share of GDP. If one assumes, as a first approximation, that the share of nontradables is about the same across the sample and that bank loans are evenly distributed across the economy, then DLD offers a plausible ranking of currency-denomination mismatch: the larger is DLD, the larger will be the mismatch. The chapter also shows that integration with the global capital market has an effect on the probability of SS, but the sign depends on how deep is the financial integration. For economies that are weakly integrated, increasing capital market integration *increases* the probability of SS. EMs are in that group. In contrast, if integration is already large, the effect is negative: increasing capital market integration *lowers* the probability of SS. DMs are in that group.[1]

All this makes intuitive sense. The existence of a large CAD could involve financial vulnerabilities, especially under incomplete financial markets, because the larger is CAD, the more likely one would expect it to be the financial disarray (e.g., bankruptcies) caused by the fall in aggregate demand associated with SS. On the one hand, in a systemic financial tightening situation, the larger is CAD, the larger the incentives for investors to "wait and see," activating domestic financial vulnerabilities (e.g., bankruptcies) that give rise to domestic SS. Notice that the materialization of SS may just be the result of self-fulfilling expectations. DLD, on the other hand, can have similar disruptive effects, unless the government has sufficient international reserves to soften the blow.[2] Incidentally, DLD does not include external debt. This was motivated by Argentina's 2001 crisis, which suggests that banking crises are all the more disruptive if they seriously interfere with the *domestic* payments system. Paralyzing the payments system stops the economy on its tracks and is more likely to give rise to SS. Interestingly, once DLD is included as an explanatory variable, other popular variables like short-term foreign exchange denominated debt are not statistically significant. This does not deny their relevance for exacerbating the effects of financial crises but questions their relevance for explaining extreme episodes like SS, once DLD is taken into account.

Moreover CAD and DLD may interact during a SS episode. A shock that entails a fall in CAD is likely to trigger real depreciation of the currency, namely an increase in the relative price of tradables in terms of nontradables. The financial disruption this brings about is likely to be larger, the larger is the currency-denomination mismatch, DLD. This nonlinearity is borne out by the empirical results in the paper. Finally, financial integration, if at all significant, has to increase the probability of SS; by definition, if international financial integration is nonexistent, SS cannot occur. Thus, in the early stages of financial integration, the latter must enhance the probability of SS. However, a deeply integrated economy is likely to have available a variety of financial instruments for offsetting financial stringency or, at least, for ameliorating its impact and lowering the probability of SS.[3]

A key result in the chapter, based on panel data, is that the time dummy varies substantially across systemic SS episodes. The importance of this fact became evident in Calvo, Izquierdo, and Loo-Kung (2013), a study that employs the results in chapter 7 to estimate the stock of international reserves that would be optimal for preventing SS. Depending on the time dummy (which appears to be positively correlated with the virulence of the systemic shock), optimal reserves for a given economy could be nil or, say, 40 percent of GDP. In our sample, the largest optimal reserve stocks are recorded for 1997, the year prior to the virulent 1998 Russian crisis (as discussed in chapter 1). These results highlight the relevance of the liquidity approach, which, in line with the discussion in chapter 2, suggests that Knightian (1921) uncertainty reigns supreme. This is disappointing for the policy maker who expects research to provide ironclad results, but it would be wrong to conclude that these results are of no use. In the first place, results are relevant for risk-averse policy makers, especially those adopting value-at-risk strategies, or that fear the politically devastating implications usually associated with a SS episode. Moreover results are relevant in situations in which, for considerations outside the model, policy makers have a good sense of the probability of a systemic crisis.

Despite these limitations, findings in chapter 7 suggest that macro policy in EMs, like accumulating of international reserves, eschewing currency mismatch, paring down large current account deficits and implementing either limited or extensive financial integration with the rest of the world, can help lower the probability of SS in a 3S episode. This is significant progress if one endorses the view, conjectured in this book, that, in the present state of the arts, systemic financial crises have large unknown and/or random components.

6 Systemic Sudden Stops: Crises and Recoveries in EMs

Guillermo Calvo and Pablo Ottonello

Systemic Sudden Stops (3S) in EMs have effects akin to liquidity crunch. In this chapter we define and characterize economic crises associated with those shocks, and discuss the differences and similarities with "regular" recession episodes in EMs.

Perhaps the most striking feature of 3S crises is that their recovery is not accompanied by a surge of external or domestic credit stocks and flows, even though, by constructions, those episodes involve a major credit contraction.[1] This is in sharp contrast with regular recession episodes in which consumption smoothing appears to be the rule, and reinforces the view that a major liquidity shock is at stake.

The 3S episodes we discuss are associated with significantly larger output contractions than regular recessions, and longer recoveries than for regular recessions. The recoveries may reflect the long time needed for liquidity reconstruction after a liquidity crunch. Moreover, the lack of credit recovery increases social welfare cost, given that it forces a major fall in aggregate expenditure, a painful adjustment, especially if economies start from current account deficit (the typical case).

Another interesting feature is that 3S crises involve sharp and persistent changes in key relative prices such as the real wage and real exchange rate. On average, peak to trough, the real wage falls by almost 10 percent, while the real exchange rate rises by over 40 percent, and show little recovery. In regular recessions, the real wage falls by only around 2 percent and fully recovers with output, and the real exchange rate is virtually flat. The persistent adjustment of real wages during 3S episodes is mostly observed during episodes with high inflation, and can be a key element behind the recovery of employment during 3S episodes. In fact, most of output fluctuations during 3S episodes can be accounted by changes in measured total factor productivity or by capacity utilization.

Demand-side components also show significant differences. Investment and imports are the main casualties in 3S crises. On average, peak to trough, investment contracts around 5 percentage points of GDP, while in regular recession episodes investment contraction is only around 1 percent. The contraction of investment during 3S episodes also displays significant persistence. On the external side, in regular recessions imports and exports show an upward trend over the entire peak-to-recovery cycle. Exports in 3S also show an upward trend but the slope is much larger than in regular recessions. However, this is not enough to offset the credit crunch, and imports are forced to fall. Finally, in contrast to regular recession episodes, 3S crises shows little consumption smoothing, with consumption mimicking the behavior of output.

Methodology

We construct a sample of recession episodes associated with 3S, and a sample of "regular" recession episodes. Natural candidates to study 3S episodes are countries that are integrated into the world capital market. The sample is composed of the set of countries that are tracked by JP Morgan in its global Emerging Market Bond Index, or global EMBI, with observations spanning the period 1980 to 2006.[2]

Employing annual data, we identify the beginning of a recession episode with a contraction of output (measured by GDP divided by working-age population). For each recession episode we define a corresponding peak, trough, and recovery point (see appendix B for details).

If the peak-to-trough window of a recession episode has an intersection with a 3S window, the recession episode is classified as a 3S crisis. We define a 3S window following Calvo, Izquierdo, and Loo-Kung (2006), as the union of:

• a capital-flow window containing a fall in capital flows for a given country exceeding two standard deviations from its mean (that starts when the fall in capital flows exceeds one standard deviation, and ends when it is smaller than one standard deviation) that overlaps at any point in time with
• a window containing a spike in the aggregate EMBI spread exceeding two standard deviations, from its mean (which starts when the aggregate EMBI spread exceeds one standard deviation, and ends when it is smaller than one standard deviation).[3]

This classification yields a group of 32 recession episodes that contains most of the well-known crises throughout the 1980s and 1990s, including the Latin American Debt Crisis episodes (Argentina 1981, Brazil 1981, Chile 1982, Mexico 1982, Uruguay 1982, Venezuela 1981), the Tequila crisis episodes (Argentina 1995, Mexico 1995, Turkey 1994), the East Asian crisis episodes (Indonesia 1998, Korea 1998, Malaysia

1998, Thailand 1997), and the Russian crisis episodes of the late 1990s (Ecuador 1999, Turkey 1999, Argentina 1999). Table C1 of appendix C provides a complete list of 3S recession episodes.

To put the dynamics of 3S recession episodes in perspective, we construct a set of benchmark "regular" recession episodes, in which financial factors were not a central element of the recession. Within recession episodes not classified as 3S crises, we define a regular recession episode as one in which no banking crisis, or no debt default/rescheduling event occurs in a window from one year before the output per capita peak to one year after the output per capita recovery point.[4] Given the frequency with which financial crises occur in EMs (73 percent of the recession episodes of our sample feature a financial crisis episode), the sample of regular recessions includes only 17 episodes. Table C1 of appendix C provides the list of regular recession episodes.

Sudden Stop and Bank Credit Flows

The first defining element of a 3S crisis is the current account adjustment experienced during the recession episode. Panel a of figure 6.1 shows that in the average 3S crisis the current account exhibits a severe adjustment and increases 6 percentage points of GDP from output peak-to-trough (significant at the 1 percent level; see appendix C). This adjustment is in sharp contrast with the average regular recession episode, in which the current account exhibits a slight *deterioration*, which would be consistent with expenditure smoothing.

In the recovery phase of the episode, the current account of 3S crises exhibits a slight reversal, around 30 percent of its

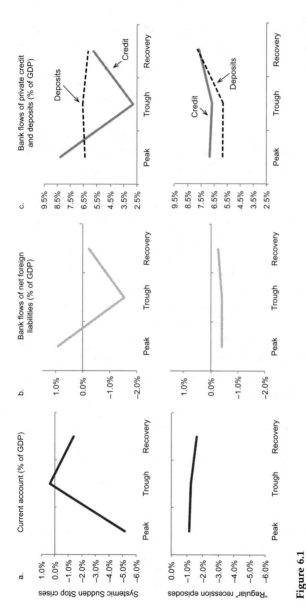

Figure 6.1
Current account (a) and bank flows (b–c). Figures show the average Systemic Sudden Stop crisis and the average "regular" recession episode at the recession peak, trough, and recovery point. Sample, variables definitions, and data sources are detailed in appendixes A and B.

adjustment from peak to trough. As a consequence, once output recovers its trend, the current account is still almost 4 percentage points of GDP above its output-peak levels (significant at the 1 percent level). Given that one of the defining elements of 3S crises is the abrupt interruption of external credit, it is quite striking that the economy is able to recover without much recovery of external credit. For this reason, Calvo, Izquierdo, and Talvi (2006) label these episodes "Phoenix Miracles," in the sense that output seems to be "rising from its ashes."

Banks do not seem to be immune to the sudden stop. Panels b and c show that they experience a "bank run" stemming from a sharp decline in banks foreign liabilities—not bank deposits. Banks net foreign liabilities exhibit a contraction of 2 percentage points of GDP from peak to trough, which is equivalent to 38 percent of their deposit flows at the output peak (significant at the 1 percent level). Deposit flows, in contrast, remain stable during the whole episode, not changing significantly from the output peak. The other side of the coin of the sudden stop in banks' net foreign liabilities is the dramatic collapse of bank credit flows to the private sector. In particular, panel b shows that bank credit flows to the private sector contract by 5 percentage points of GDP from peak to trough (significant at the 5 percent level). The behavior of bank flows is in sharp contrast with regular recession episodes in which bank net foreign liabilities remain roughly unchanged and bank credit flows to the private sector do not experience a severe contraction from output peak to trough. Moreover, in 3S episodes, once output recovers its trend, banks' net foreign liabilities and credit flows to the private sector remain below their pre-crisis level (significant at the 5 percent level), recovering 54 percent its peak-to-trough contraction. Therefore, both from the perspective of external and domestic credit, 3S crises exhibit a precarious recovery of flows.

Relative Prices

Figure 6.2 depicts the dynamics of two key relative prices: the real wage and the real exchange rate.[5] Panel a shows that, in contrast with regular recession episodes, during 3S crises real wages contract on average by 11 percent from output peak to trough, and remain on average 7 percent below their pre-crisis level at the time that output recovers its trend (the change from peak to trough is significant at the 1 percent level; the change from peak to recovery is significant at the 5 percent level). Calvo, Coricelli, and Ottonello (2012) provide empirical evidence showing that inflation is a key ingredient to understand the pattern of recovery in real wages during financial crises. To illustrate this point in our sample, figure 6.2 splits the sample of 3S crises into high- and low-inflation episodes.[6] Results indicate that the adjustment in real wages occurs mostly in high-inflation episodes, suggesting the presence of nominal wage rigidity.[7] Calvo, Coricelli, and Ottonello (2012) show that this adjustment in wages is an important component in helping unemployment to return to its pre-crisis level. In financial crises with low inflation, real wages do not significantly adjust and unemployment remains above its pre-crisis level once output recovers its trend, displaying "jobless recovery." The authors show that this pattern of labor recovery from financial crises is consistent with a simple model in which collateral requirements are higher (lower) when a larger share of labor costs (physical capital expenditure) is involved in a loan contract. In this framework, the partial recovery of credit documented in the preceding section

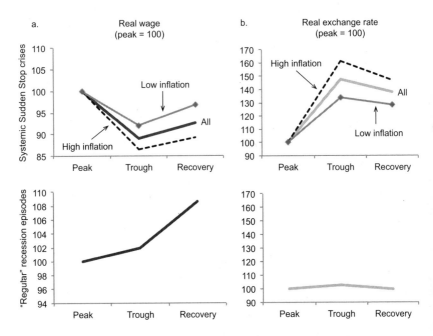

Figure 6.2
Real wage (a) and the real exchange rate (b). Figures show the average
Systemic Sudden Stop crisis and the average "regular" recession episode at
the recession peak, trough, and recovery point. An increase in the real
exchange rate denotes is equivalent to real currency depreciation. High
inflation (low inflation) denotes the set of episodes in which the maximum
level of annual CPI inflation during the episode was above (below) 30
percent. Sample, variables definitions, and data sources are detailed in
appendixes A and B.

would be a central factor for explaining sluggish recovery
of real wages during 3S crises.

Panel b shows that the dynamics of the real exchange rate
also depicts a remarkably different behavior in 3S crises than
in regular recession episodes. In particular, in 3S crises the
real exchange rate shoots up by about 43 percent from peak
to trough (and this increase is significant at the 1 percent
level), and remains on average 39 percent above its pre-crisis

level once output recovers its trend (significant at the 1 percent level).[8] This fact is one of the key points regarding Sudden Stops and systemic crises made in Calvo, Izquierdo, and Talvi (2003), stressing the impact of a sudden collapse in external financing of the current account deficit over the real exchange rate. It is interesting to note that low-inflation episodes also display significantly large and persistent real currency depreciation. Calvo, Coricelli, and Ottonello (2014) document that, in general, during EM financial crises neither the change in the real exchange rate nor the change in output composition (tradable/nontradable) from output peak to recovery tend to display a significant relationship with inflation.

Aggregate Investment, Consumption, and Exports

A key piece of evidence to understand the nature of 3S crises and their recovery can be obtained by studying the behavior of the components of aggregate expenditure. Figure 6.3 depicts the behavior of aggregate investment, consumption, exports, and imports, all relative to output.

Panel a shows that 3S crises are characterized by a dramatic fall of aggregate investment, which exceeds that of output. The collapse of aggregate investment is particularly large in 3S crises when compared to that of regular recession episodes. This contraction of investment in 3S crises is to some extent not surprising, given the key role that financial factors typically play on capital purchases. What is less obvious is why at the time of full output recovery (more than three years on average after the trough) the investment rate in these episodes is still 14 percent below its pre-crisis level, recovering less than 40 percent of its contraction (significant at the 1 percent level). This fact, first documented in Calvo,

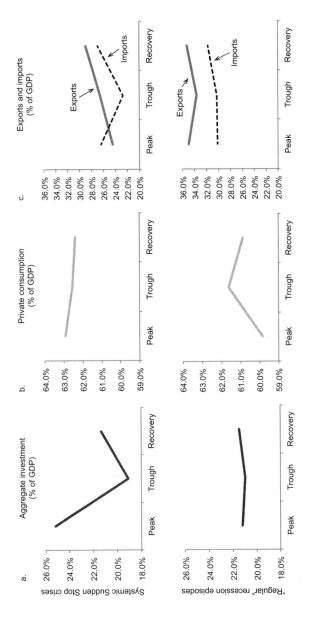

Figure 6.3
Investment (a), consumption (b), exports and imports (c). Figures show the average Systemic Sudden Stop crisis and the average "regular" recession episode at the recession peak, trough, and recovery point. Investment, consumption, exports and imports are expressed in real terms, over real GDP. Sample, variables definitions, and data sources are detailed in appendixes A and B.

Izquierdo, and Talvi (2006), has been also found in financial crises of developed market economies (e.g., see Rioja, Rios-Avila, and Valev 2014). Three main explanations can be found in the literature for this behavior of investment. First, Calvo, Izquierdo, and Talvi (2006) argue that in the absence of external or domestic credit, and if banks are the main providers of firms' working capital, lower investment makes room for working capital accumulation—which, coupled with excess capacity, leads to output recovery. A second complementary explanation is that financial crises have a persistent effect on key variables affecting investment rate of return. For instance, financial crises can have a persistent effect on the net worth of the business or financial sectors; during the recovery phase a depressed net worth can increase borrowing costs for purchasing capital (as in Bernanke and Gertler 1989; Bernanke, Gertler, and Gilchrist 1999). Alternatively, financial crises can lead to a large share of capital "unemployment" (e.g., structures not matched to a business and searching to be reallocated), which decreases the rate of return on the production of new capital goods (Ottonello 2014). A third possible explanation is that 3S crises could have a persistent effect on uncertainty, for instance, through the policy environment.[9] Increases in uncertainty can lead firms to adopt wait-and-see strategies and maintain low levels of investment (e.g., see Bloom, Bond, and Van Reenen 2007; Stokey 2013).

Panel b shows that in the average 3S financial crisis episode private consumption roughly mimics the behavior of output (peak-to-trough, trough-to-recovery, and peak-to-recovery changes are not significant at the 10 percent level). This pattern of private consumption is qualitatively different than in the average regular recession episode, in which consumption tends to fall less than output, as one would expect from simple consumption-smoothing theory. Two main explanations have been provided in the literature for this behavior of consumption. The first explanation is that Sudden Stops are periods of tightening of borrowing constraints (e.g., following liquidity crunch), which limit the possibility of consumption smoothing (e.g., see Calvo 1998; Mendoza 2010; Bianchi 2011). The second is that the shocks perceived by the economy during the sudden stop episode (such as interest rate shocks or nonstationary productivity shocks) make it optimal to significantly contract consumption (see Neumeyer and Perri 2005; Uribe and Yue 2006; Aguiar and Gopinath 2007).

Panel c shows that 3S episodes are characterized by a significant increase of exports relative to output (significant at the 1 percent level). Given that imports first collapse (the 14 percent drop from peak-to-trough recovery is significant at the one percent level) and then recover their pre-crisis level (the change from peak-to-recovery is not significantly different from zero at the 10 percent level), net exports significantly increase following 3S financial crisis episodes, which is consistent with the pattern exhibited by the current account and the real exchange rate in previous sections. As discussed in these sections, this pattern is not observed in regular recession episodes.

Output Dynamics

Figure 6.4, panel a, depicts the dynamics of output per capita during the typical 3S financial crisis episode, characterized by two key features. First, 3S crises tend to display large output contractions, 11 percent on average from output peak to trough. The magnitude of this contraction is five times larger than the one experienced in regular recession

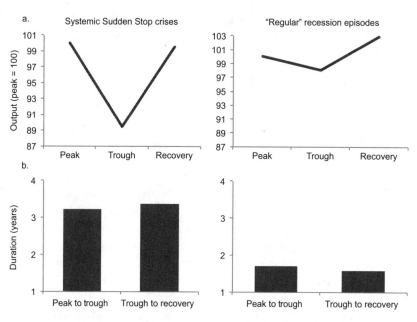

Figure 6.4
Output dynamics. Figures show the average Systemic Sudden Stop crisis and the average "regular" recession episode at the recession peak, trough, and recovery point. (a) Output is expressed in real terms, over the working-age population. (b) The duration from output peak to trough (trough to recovery) is the number of years between the recession peak and tough (trough and recovery). Sample, variables definitions, and data sources are detailed in appendixes A and B.

episodes (2 percent, on average, from peak to trough). This fact is consistent with other empirical studies showing that financial crises are typically associated with a larger output contraction than other recession episodes (see Reinhart and Rogoff 2009). The second fact, documented in panel b is that 3S financial crisis episodes tend to display a large duration. From output peak to recovery these episodes last 6.6 years on average, which compares to 3.3 years average duration of regular recession episodes. Queralto (2015) and Saffie and Ates (2013) construct endogenous growth models to explain slow recoveries following financial crises.

The duration of recessions following 3S episodes is also consistent with the view that liquidity crunch episodes have effects on the output trend. Cerra and Saxena (2008), for instance, provide evidence supporting the view that financial crises have a permanent effect on output. As argued in Calvo, Izquierdo, and Talvi (2006), a stagnation of trend growth during financial crises is not an implausible outcome: during a phase of dramatic financial disarray, firms are likely to devote much of their attention to the re-composition of their financing, paying little attention to increasing factor productivity.[10] Midrigan and Xu (2014) provide evidence of an important related channel: financial crises can distort entry and technology adoption decisions and thus reduce productivity of individual producers. Additionally Kehoe and Prescott (2007) argue that negative policy changes that affect productivity tend to occur during large crisis episodes, such as 3S crises.

Employment, Capital, and Measured TFP

A key piece of evidence to understand the larger output contraction and its persistence during 3S crises can be obtained by conducting a growth accounting exercise. Figure 6.5 illustrates this exercise, depicting the behavior of capital, employment, and measured total factor productivity (TFP) — computed according to standard growth accounting.[11]

This exercise reveals that TFP is the central element driving the dynamics of output: Variations in TFP account for the bulk of the variation in output throughout the

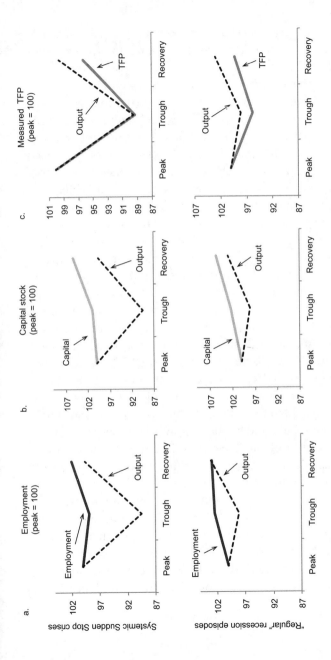

Figure 6.5
Employment (a), capital (b), and measured TFP (c). Figure shows the average Systemic Sudden Stop crisis and the average "regular" recession episode at the recession peak, trough, and recovery point. Output, capital, and employment are expressed in real terms, over the working-age population. Sample, variables definitions, and data sources are detailed in appendixes A and B.

collapse–recovery process. In particular, TFP falls sharply during the contraction phase, accounting for roughly the total fall from peak to trough in output per capita, and significantly recovers by the time of output reaches its pre-crisis levels, accounting for most of the increase from trough to recovery in output per capita.[12] Employment also follows a pattern similar to that of output, but it only accounts for a small fraction of the variation in output relative to TFP. The capital stock depicts a moderate increase during the whole episode, having little role explaining collapse–recovery dynamics.

Regular recession episodes in EMs are also characterized by a contraction of TFP that accounts for most of the variations of output during these episodes. However, the contraction of TFP during 3S crises is larger and more persistent than in regular recession episodes. The central role of TFP found in the dynamics of 3S crises can be also found in the US Great Depression and other large economic crises in developed market economies (see Cole and Ohanian 1999; Calvo et al. 2006; Kehoe and Prescott 2007). These large swings in measured TFP are hard to attribute to technological factors. Several alternative explanations have been provided in the literature. First, Calvo, Izquierdo, and Talvi (2006) argue that sudden changes in TFP, as measured, are missing a central element, which is the effect of a credit disarray on capacity utilization. In this line, Mendoza (2006) and Meza and Quintin (2007) show that capital utilization and labor hoarding can be quantitatively relevant to account for the drop of measured TFP following a Sudden Stop. A second possible explanation is that changes in measured TFP stem from factor misallocation among heterogeneous firms induced by credit disarray, which can show up as an efficiency wedge (e.g., see Shourideh and Zetlin-Jones 2012;

Chen and Song 2013; Khan and Thomas 2013; Buera and Moll 2015). Oberfield (2013) and Sandleris and Wright (2014) provide empirical support to this view for EM sudden stop episodes. Third, financial factors can affect the use or efficiency of intermediate inputs (see Mendoza 2010; Pratap and Urrutia 2012), which would also show up as measured TFP. Gopinath and Neiman (2013) provide empirical evidence related to this mechanism.

Conclusions

Episodes of Systemic Sudden Stops (3S) in EMs have proved to be useful for obtaining empirical evidence on the macroeconomic dynamics following phenomena akin to liquidity crunch. The following facts are central characteristics of 3S recession episodes:

• 3S are associated with large and persistent output collapses.
• Most of the contraction of output and its persistence during 3S crises are not driven by changes of employment and capital, but by changes in measured total factor productivity.
• Although the contraction of external and domestic credit flows is the proximate cause of the output collapse, output recovery occurs with only a partial recovery of these credit flows.
• These episodes are associated with pronounced and persistent changes of relative prices (real wages and real exchange rate), especially in high-inflation episodes.
• Finally, the collapse of output occurs with little consumption smoothing and a large and persistent collapse of aggregate investment; a larger share of output is absorbed as net exports throughout episode.

The picture that emerges is that disruptions in credit markets seem to be associated with a large adjustment of economic activity, expenditure, and relative prices. In economies where relative prices—and, in particular, real wages—are able to adjust, the recovery of credit flows is not a necessary condition for output, employment, and consumption recovery to pre-crisis levels. However, there is a price to pay in that return to trend is long-winded when at all possible.

Appendixes

Appendix A   Data

The following data were used to construct the figures of this chapter (for each variable, subscript i denotes the country and t denotes the time period):

1. Real GDP per capita (y_{it}^{pc}): obtained from World Development Indicators (WDI).
2. GDP in local currency (Y_{it}): obtained from WDI
3. GDP in US dollars (Y_{it}^*): obtained from WDI.
4. Working age population ratio (n_{it}^{wa}): population aged 15–64 over total population, obtained from World Development Indicators (WDI).
5. Real GDP over working-age-population (y_{it}): constructed as

$$y_{it} = y_{it}^{pc} \times n_{it}^{wa}.$$

6. Current account over GDP: obtained from WDI and World Economic Outlook (WEO).
7. Bank net foreign liabilities (NFL_{it}^*): obtained from International Monetary Fund (IMF), measured as the

difference between foreign liabilities and foreign assets in US dollars of Other Depository Corporations.

8. Bank credit to the private sector (B_{it}): obtained from IMF, measured as claims on the private sector of "Other Depository Corporations."

9. Bank deposits (D_{it}): obtained from IMF, measured as demand deposits, time, savings, and foreign currency deposits of Other Depository Corporations.

10. Bank net foreign liability flows over GDP ($fnfly_{it}$): constructed as

$$fnfly_{it} = \frac{NFL^*_{i,t} - NFL^*_{i,t-1}}{Y^*_{i,t}}.$$

11. Bank credit flows to the private sector over GDP (fby_{it}): constructed as

$$fby_{it} = \frac{B_{i,t} - B_{i,t-1}}{Y_{i,t}}.$$

12. Bank deposit flows over GDP (fdy_{it}): constructed as

$$fdy_{it} = \frac{D_{i,t} - D_{i,t-1}}{Y_{i,t}}.$$

13. Nominal wages (W_{it}): obtained from International Labor Organization (ILO), Economic Commission for Latin America (ECLA), Trading Economics, and from national sources.

14. Producer price index (P^p_{it}): IMF and national sources.

15. Wholesale price index (P^w_{it}): obtained from IMF and national sources.

16. Consumer price index (P^c_{it}): obtained from WDI and WEO.

17. Nominal exchange rate (E_{it}): obtained from WDI and WEO, expressed as units of local currency per US dollar.

18. Real wage (w_{it}): constructed as

$$w_{it} = \frac{W_{it}}{P_{it}^{p}}.$$

For countries in which P_{it}^{p} was not available, P_{it}^{w} or P_{it}^{c} were used.

19. Real exchange rate (rxr_{it}): constructed as

$$rxr_{it} = \frac{E_{it}P_{us,t}^{c}}{P_{it}^{c}},$$

where $P_{us,t}^{c}$ denotes the consumer price index in the United States.

20. Real consumption over GDP (cy_{it}): obtained from WDI, measured as constant final consumption expenditure over constant GDP, in local currency.

21. Real investment over GDP (iy_{it}): obtained from WDI, measured as constant gross capital formation over constant GDP, in local currency.

22. Real exports over GDP (xy_{it}): obtained from WDI, measured as constant exports of goods and services over constant GDP, in local currency.

23. Real imports over GDP (imy_{it}): obtained from WDI, measured as constant imports of goods and services over constant GDP, in local currency.

24. Real capital stock per capita (k_{it}^{pc}): obtained from Penn World Table, version 8.0; Feenstra, Inklaar and Timmer (2013), "The Next Generation of the Penn World Table" available for download at www.ggdc.net/pwt.

25. Employment per capita (l_{it}^{pc}): obtained from Penn World Table and WEO.

26. Capital share (α_{it}): obtained from Penn World Table.

27. Measured total factor productivity ($\hat{a}_{it}$): constructed as

$$\hat{a}_{it} = \frac{y_{it}}{k_{it}^{\alpha_i} l_{it}^{1-\alpha_i}},$$

where α_i is the average capital share for country i.

Figure 6.1 uses data from time series 6, 10, 11, and 12; figure 6.2 from time series 18 and 19; figure 6.3 from time series 20, 21, 22, and 23; figure 6.4 from time series 5; figure 6.5 from time series 5, 24, 25, and 27.

All variables are obtained or constructed at the annual frequency from 1980 to 2007. As explained in the chapter, the study includes data for 27 EM economies integrated to global capital markets: Algeria, Argentina, Brazil, Bulgaria, Chile, Colombia, Dominican Republic, Ecuador, El Salvador, Indonesia, Ivory Coast, Lebanon, Malaysia, Mexico, Morocco, Nigeria, Panama, Peru, Philippines, Russia, South Africa, South Korea, Thailand, Tunisia, Turkey, Uruguay, and Venezuela.

Appendix B   Sample

The main objective of the empirical analysis is to study the macroeconomic dynamics during a recession episode following a systemic sudden stop. To this end, we build a sample of recession episodes in EMs and define, for each recession episode, an output peak, trough, and a recovery point. The beginning of recession event is identified by a period of contraction of output, measured by real GDP over working-age-population (time series 5 in appendix A). For each recession episode, we define a peak, trough, and recovery point. The peak is the time period preceding the initial output contraction that identifies the recession episode. The recovery point is defined as the period in which output recovers its trend level. The cyclical component of output was computed using HP filter, with a smoothing parameter of 100. If there is one year or less between the recovery from a recession episode and the peak of the following recession, we consider these a single recession episode (to capture "double-deep" recession episodes). Since we are interested in analyzing the recovery in market economies, we excluded from this sample episodes associated with the dissolution of the Soviet Union (in particular, the recession episodes that started prior to 1991 in Bulgaria and Russia). With this methodology we identify 83 recession episodes for the period 1980 to 2007.

If the peak-to-trough window of a recession episode has an intersection with the 3S window, the recession episode is classified as a "Systemic Sudden Stop crisis." This classification yields a group of 32 systemic sudden stop crises (3S crises) detailed in table C1. To put the dynamics of 3S crises in perspective, we construct a set of benchmark "regular" recession episodes, in which financial factors were not a central element of the recession. Within the set of recession episodes which are not 3S crises, we define a regular recession episode as one in which no banking crisis, or no debt default/rescheduling event occurs in a window from 1 year before the output per capita peak to 1 year after the output per capita recovery point. Data on banking crises and debt default/rescheduling are from Reinhart and Rogoff (2009). This classification yields a group of 17 recession episodes detailed in table C1.

Appendix C Statistical Tests

In this section present the results of the statistical tests mentioned in the chapter, which provide more evidence on the stylized facts documented in the chapter through the behavior of the average 3S crisis episode (depicted in figures 6.1 through 6.5). We test whether changes in the variables of interest during 3S crises are different from zero, by regressing them on a constant. Column 1 reports the estimated coefficients for the change of variables between the recession peak and trough, column 2 for the change between trough and recovery, and column 3 for the change between peak and recovery.

Table C1
Sample of recession episodes

3S Crises		Regular recession episodes	
Country	Peak	Country	Peak
Algeria	1999	Algeria	1980
Argentina	1980	Algeria	2005
Argentina	1994	Argentina	1984
Argentina	1998	Colombia	1990
Brazil	1980	Colombia	1992
Brazil	1995	Dominican Republic	1987
Brazil	1997	Dominican Republic	1989
Chile	1981	Ecuador	1986
Chile	1998	Ecuador	1991
Colombia	1997	Indonesia	1981
Dominican Republic	1981	Morocco	1988

Table C1 (continued)

3S Crises		Regular recession episodes	
Country	Peak	Country	Peak
Ecuador	1981	Panama	1994
Ecuador	1998	Panama	2000
El Salvador	1980	Philippines	1990
Indonesia	1997	South Africa	1997
Ivory Coast	1980	Tunisia	2001
Korea	1997	Uruguay	1994
Lebanon	1996		
Malaysia	1997		
Mexico	1981		
Mexico	1994		
Morocco	1980		
Morocco	1991		
Peru	1997		
Philippines	1982		
Philippines	1997		
Thailand	1996		
Tunisia	1981		
Turkey	1993		
Turkey	1998		
Uruguay	1981		
Venezuela	1980		

Table C2
Statistical tests

		(1) Peak to trough: i=peak j=trough	(2) Trough to recovery: i=trough j=recovery	(3) Peak to recovery: i=peak j=recovery	Number of observations
Current account	$\Delta_{i\text{-}j}ca_j$	0.055*** (0.012	-0.018** (0.008)	0.038*** (0.011)	30
Bank net foreign liability flows	$\Delta_{i\text{-}j}fnfly_j$	-0.024*** (0.009)	0.013* (0.007)	-0.012* (0.006)	30
Bank credit to private sector	$\Delta_{i\text{-}j}fby_j$	-0.055** (0.020)	0.029* (0.016)	-0.025** (0.012)	31
Bank deposit to private sector	$\Delta_{i\text{-}j}fdy_j$	0.002 (0.011)	-0.004 (0.010)	-0.002 (0.006)	31
Real wage	$\Delta_{i\text{-}j}\log(w_j)$	-0.144*** (0.046)	0.004 (0.029)	-0.100** (0.042)	27
Real exchange rate	$\Delta_{i\text{-}j}\log(rxr_j)$	0.344*** (0.052)	-0.073* (0.036)	0.271*** (0.055)	32
Investment over GDP	$\Delta_{i\text{-}j}\log(iy_j)$	-0.281*** (0.040)	0.134*** (0.032)	-0.147*** (0.042)	31
Consumption over GDP	$\Delta_{i\text{-}j}\log(cy_j)$	-0.005 (0.012)	-0.004 (0.011)	-0.009 (0.014)	30
Exports over GDP	$\Delta_{i\text{-}j}\log(xy_j)$	0.140*** (0.037)	0.072*** (0.017)	0.212*** (0.040)	32
Imports over GDP	$\Delta_{i\text{-}j}\log(imy_j)$	-0.194*** (0.035)	0.185*** (0.035)	-0.008 (0.039)	31
Output	$\Delta_{i\text{-}j}\log(y_j)$	-0.116*** (0.018)	0.106*** (0.014)	-0.010 (0.020)	32
Capital	$\Delta_{i\text{-}j}\log(k_j)$	0.005 (0.018)	0.038*** (0.011)	0.043* (0.025)	31
Employment	$\Delta_{i\text{-}j}\log(e_j)$	-0.013 (0.009)	0.030** (0.013)	0.017 (0.013)	30
Measured TFP	$\Delta_{i\text{-}j}\log(\hat{a}_j)$	-0.116*** (0.014)	0.076*** (0.010)	-0.040*** (0.014)	29

Note: Standard errors in parentheses. Each estimated coefficient was obtained from a separate regression of the variable of interest on a constant. * indicates significance at 10 percent level, ** at 5 percent level, *** at 1 percent level. Sample and variables definition are detailed in appendixes A and B.

7 Systemic Sudden Stops: The Relevance of Balance-Sheet Effects and Financial Integration

Guillermo Calvo, Alejandro Izquierdo, and Luis-Fernando Mejía

Our central objective in this chapter is to try to isolate the role of domestic financial factors, and in particular, the role of foreign-exchange denominated debts and financial integration into world capital markets. Although our approach is mostly empirical, we use a theoretical background to establish potential changes in the real exchange rate and their balance-sheet effects. The Sudden Stops episodes that we mainly discuss are episodes in which the economy exhibits a "large and largely unexpected" cut in capital inflows. We also extend our discussion to Systemic Sudden Stops (3S), which, you may recall, are sudden stops that take place in conjunction with a sharp rise in aggregate interest-rate spreads.

It has been claimed for these episodes that the initial trigger is *financial and external*. The procedure we use to select Sudden Stop episodes is designed to exclude crises that are idiosyncratic and can be due to factors quite disparate (natural disasters, political turmoil, etc.) from the purely financial crises that we intend to isolate. Moreover, since our crisis definition tries to isolate episodes that are "largely unexpected," it could be argued that in these episodes market incompleteness is likely to prevail, making shocks such as large changes in relative prices difficult to handle in a context of noncontingent contracts.

The simple model discussed in in the next section captures these characteristics. In it we assume that 3S are initially triggered by factors that are exogenous to individual economies. However, whether or not this initial shock develops into a full-fledged Sudden Stop depends on country-specific variables. We conjecture that foreign-currency denominated debts play a central role when the Sudden Stop brings about a sharp increase in the real exchange rate. This is so because central banks have serious limitations as lenders of last resort in terms of foreign exchange. In the empirical implementation we focus on an even narrower concept of foreign-exchange denominated debt, namely *domestic liability dollarization* (DLD), that is to say, foreign-exchange denominated *domestic* debts toward the *domestic banking system*, as a share of GDP. The rationale behind this choice is that typically banks are at the heart of the economy's *payment system,* and thus their bankruptcy or even temporary suspension of activities can trigger a serious supply shock. The crises we consider are in many instances associated with major real currency depreciation. Thus we found it necessary to bring into focus factors that could provoke large increases in the real exchange rate. The framework introduced below shows that a key factor is the current account deficit *as a share of absorption of tradable goods*, which is shown to be negatively related to the ratio of tradables' output (net of transfers) to tradables' absorption (a variable that we denote by ω, as explained below).[2] The smaller is ω, the larger will be the impact on tradables' absorption of a Sudden Stop (keeping international reserves constant), and thus the larger its impact on the real exchange rate. The model leads us to expect that the probability of a Sudden Stop will be negatively associated with ω and positively associated with DLD (given the exogenous financial trigger), bringing to the forefront the relevance of potential balance-sheet effects on the likelihood of a Sudden Stop.

Basic Framework

We consider here cases in which it can be argued that the initial shock is systemic and associated with a sharp increase in the cost of credit, initially inducing substantial contraction in international credit and aggregate demand. Whether or not this initial credit contraction results in a full-fledged Sudden Stop depends on the effects of the initial contraction, which in turn depend on domestic vulnerabilities.

Let us take two sectors: tradables and nontradables. The demand function for nontradables is

$$h = \alpha + \beta \, rer + \delta \, z, \tag{1}$$

where $h = \log H$, $z = \log Z$, $rer = \log RER$, H and Z are the demand for nontradables (or home goods) and tradables, RER is the real exchange rate (i.e., the relative price of tradables with respect to nontradables), and α, β, and δ are parameters, $\beta > 0$, $\delta > 0$.[3] Suppose, for simplicity, that the supply of tradables and nontradables is inelastically given. By equation (1), if z contracts by Δz, in equilibrium we have

$$\Delta rer = -\frac{\delta}{\beta} \, \Delta z, \tag{2}$$

where Δ is the first-difference operator. Clearly, the larger is the proportional contraction of the demand for tradables, the larger will be the proportional increase in the real exchange rate. Changes in rer in turn change the ratio of foreign-exchange denominated debt to GDP (assuming that those debts are not state-contingent, which is justified by looking at episodes where capital flow cuts are large and can be presumed to be largely unexpected). Thus, given a positive stock of foreign-exchange denominated debt, the larger Δrer, the larger will be the probability of financial distress. This illustrates how a systemic financial shock could create financial domestic distress, especially if the foreign-denominated debt is owed to domestic banks, as noted in the Introduction.[4]

The next step is to trace the effect of credit contraction on z. It should be clear from the start that such an effect will depend on preexisting debt maturity structure and central bank policy with respect to international reserves, subjects that we do not address here. Instead, the ensuing discussion suggests that a plausible proxy for the initial impact of a credit drought is the ratio of the prior-to-shock current account deficit to the absorption of tradable goods. Let the current account deficit, capital inflows, and international reserves be denoted by CAD, KI, and R, respectively. By definition, and abstracting from errors and omissions, we have

$$KI = CAD + \Delta R = Z - Y + S + \Delta R, \qquad (3)$$

where Y is output of tradables and S are international factor payments, remittances abroad, and so on. Let us focus on the case in which the initial or *incipient* Sudden Stop results in zero capital inflows, that is, $KI = 0$. If CAD remains constant (and positive), then, by equation (3), $\Delta R < 0$, driving the economy into a balance-of-payments crisis beyond which the whole adjustment will have to fall upon CAD. Hence there will come a time at which CAD will have to be set equal to zero. In the plausible case in which the economy initially attempts to honor its external financial obligations (i.e., S remains largely constant), the most favorable case is that in which Y does not contract as a result of the credit drought. In this case we have

$$\Delta Z = - CAD, \tag{4}$$

so that

$$- \Delta Z / Z = CAD / Z. \tag{5}$$

Approximating the relative change in Z by its first difference in logs, it follows from equations (2) and (5) that

$$\Delta rer = \frac{\delta}{\beta} \frac{CAD}{Z} \tag{6}$$

Thus, by equation (6), the potential proportional change in the real exchange rate increases with CAD prior to the Sudden Stop, as a ratio to the absorption of tradables (Z). Given that Y is unchanged—and in some Sudden Stop episodes Y falls (it never rises)— equation (6) gives a lower bound for the required proportional increase in the real exchange rate.[5] It should be emphasized that equation (6) does not model the *actual* change in the equilibrium real exchange rate but, rather, *that part of the total change that is likely to be very difficult to prevent*. We are now ready to complete the framework that will help to rationalize Sudden Stops as defined in the empirical section.

Suppose that a shock spreads from one country to other countries. Let this be due to the prevailing regulations in capital market transactions (e.g., margin calls) that are unrelated to country fundamentals. Such a possibility is discussed in Calvo (1999), where it is argued that a liquidity shock to informed investors due to adverse developments in one country[6] can trigger sales of assets from other countries in their portfolio in order to restore liquidity. Now add to this framework a set of uninformed investors who face a signal-extraction problem because they cannot observe whether sales of the informed are motivated by lower returns on projects or by the informed facing margin calls. In this context, uninformed investors may easily interpret the fact that informed investors stay out of the market for EM securities, or massive asset sales, as an indication of lower returns and decide to get rid of their holdings as well, even though the cause for informed investors' sales was due to margin calls.[7] When this occurs, a set of countries with no ties to the country at the epicenter of the crisis could be exposed to a large and unexpected liquidity shock, making their equilibrium real exchange rate rise through the mechanism discussed above. This is an example of the exogenous trigger referred to above. Thus, if, as a result, the proportional change in RER is large and the economy exhibits high DLD, massive bankruptcies could ensue, generating a full-fledged Sudden Stop.

The negative effect of a rise in RER can be rationalized in a variety of different ways. For example, models such as those of Izquierdo (1999) and of Arellano and Mendoza (2002), although they do not deal with bankruptcies, they do help rationalize the effects of changes in the RER on output via external credit contraction, where the relevant price is that of nontradable collateral relative to the tradable good being produced. Another scenario is given in Aghion, Bacchetta, and Banerjee (2001), and is close in spirit to the present discussion because it specifically analyzes the effects of liability dollarization. Aghion, Bacchetta, and Banerjee exploit the fact that with incomplete pass-through from exchange rates to domestic prices, currency depreciation impacts negatively on net worth due to the increase in the debt burden of domestic firms indebted in foreign currency, thus reducing investment by constrained firms as well as output levels in future periods. The associated fall in future money demand and consequent future currency depreciation, coupled with arbitrage in the foreign exchange rate market, imply that currency depreciation must take place in the current period as well, opening the door for expectational shocks that could push an economy into a bad (low output) equilibrium.[8,9] Therefore, given the damaging effect of real exchange rate fluctuations on balance sheets, output and repayment capacity, it can be argued that the probability of a 3S episode will be an increasing function of CAD/Z, and the degree of liability dollarization, especially domestic liability dollarization (DLD) and possibly other variables.[10] This is the central conjecture that will be put to a test in the next sections.

In closing this section, we want to point out that, following the empirical literature on these issues, we also include as an explanatory variable a measure of financial integration with the rest of the world. Interestingly, empirical results suggest that such a variable could increase the probability of Sudden Stop in the first stages of financial integration, while it could decrease the probability of Sudden Stop for highly financially integrated economies. The result is intuitively plausible given that, in the first place, to suffer from Sudden Stop, economies must exhibit *some* financial integration. Thus financial integration must, in principle, increase the probability of Sudden Stop. However, for highly financially integrated economies the latter effect could be more than offset by the existence of a better institutional framework (with better quality creditor rights), or state-contingent financial instruments which, by providing more orderly instruments for adjustment, lower the probability of Sudden Stop.

Sudden Stops: Definition and Characterization

Recent empirical literature has focused on alternative measures of crisis, whether currency crises (Frankel and Rose 1996;[11] Kaminsky and Reinhart 1999;[12] Edwards 2001;[13] Arteta 2003; Razin and Rubinstein 2004[14]) or current account reversals (Milesi-Ferretti and Razin 2000; Edwards 2003). However, to the extent that many of the recent crises were originated by credit shocks in international markets, as argued in Calvo (1999), the measure of crisis we want to consider is more closely linked to large and unexpected capital account movements rather than to measures that focus on large nominal currency fluctuations or current account reversals (along these lines, Edwards (2004) makes a relevant distinction between current account reversals and capital account reversals). Besides, current account and exchange rate behavior may be more affected by endogenous policy choices than Systemic Sudden Stops triggered by large and largely exogenous aggregate interest-rate spreads. Thus Systemic Sudden Stops may imply quite different timings for the onset of a crisis compared to exchange rate crises or current account reversals.[15]

One indicator of financial crisis that is akin to ours is the indicator advanced by Rodrik and Velasco (1999)—which draws on Radelet and Sachs (1998). In their view, financial crisis takes place when there is a sharp reversal in net private foreign capital flows.[16] However, this indicator does not attempt to capture the "unexpected" component in Sudden Stops, and it does not discriminate between episodes that may be of a domestic origin from those of a systemic (and hence largely exogenous) origin. In contrast to this approach, as well as that of Calvo, Izquierdo, and Mejia (2004), our indicator of Sudden Stop focuses on capital account reversals that coincide with sharp increases in aggregate spreads. This is done in order to pinpoint crises that are highly likely to be associated with an external trigger that is systemic in nature— namely Systemic Sudden Stops. In the present chapter we drop the requirement in Calvo, Izquierdo, and Mejia (2004) that capital account reversals coincide with a fall in output, thus reducing the potential influence of domestic factors in the definition keeping our focus on external triggers.[17]

Rothenberg and Warnock (2006) build on Calvo, Izqui-erdo, and Mejia (2004) to explore differences between capital account reversals originated in capital flow transactions attributable to nonresidents vis-à-vis those attributable to residents. They base their analysis also on the finding by Cowan and De Gregorio (2005) that for the case of Chile, much of the movement in the capital account balance is due to changes in gross flows stemming from residents. For a restricted sample of countries, Rothenberg and Warnock find that many of the net capital flow reversals are due to transac-tions made by residents, though more than half of the Sudden Stop episodes in their sample were due to transactions made by foreigners. However, their definition of Sudden Stops does not necessarily coincide with a spike in aggregate EMBI spreads, and thus may be capturing several events of a domestic nature. We do not follow this approach because our definition excludes crises of a domestic origin and also because there is insufficient data available on gross flows at a monthly frequency for the much larger sample of countries used in this study.[18]

Against this empirical background, and following Calvo (1998), we look for measures of a Sudden Stop that reflect *large* and *unexpected* falls in capital inflows, a central element in the characterization of this type of event. In order to make the concept of Sudden Stop operational, we first define a Sudden Stop as a phase that meets the following conditions:

• It contains at least one observation, in which the year-on-year fall in capital flows lies at least two standard deviations below its sample mean (this addresses the "unexpected" nature of a Sudden Stop).[19]
• The Sudden Stop phase ends once the annual change in capital flows exceeds one standard deviation below its sample mean. This will generally introduce persistence, a common fact of Sudden Stops.
• The start of a Sudden Stop phase is determined by the first time the annual change in capital flows falls one standard deviation below the mean.[20]

Notice that there is an important difference between this concept of crisis and the one used in other studies focusing on measures such as a fixed current account deficit threshold as a share of GDP. In line with the theoretical arguments outlined in the previous section, our definition accounts for the volatility of capital flow fluctuations of each particular country at each point in time in deciding whether an event is "large and unexpected." If anything, our concept of crisis includes episodes that would otherwise not qualify for crisis when using measures such as a fixed current account deficit threshold. This is because the latter would exclude many crisis episodes in developed countries in which the volatility is smaller.

To maximize the chances of detecting Sudden Stop episodes accurately, we work with monthly data, since lower frequency data may blur the beginning of these episodes.

Assessing the right timing of these episodes is relevant because, as it will become clear later on, eventual changes in the RER that may result from potential closure of the current account deficit need to be measured *before* a Sudden Stop takes place. Given that capital account information is typically not available at this frequency, we construct a capital flow proxy by netting out the trade balance from changes in foreign reserves (both net factor income and current transfers are thus included in our measure of capital flows, but since they represent mostly interest payments on long-term debt, they should not vary so substantially as to introduce significant spurious volatility into our capital flows measure).[21] Changes in the 12-month cumulative measure of the capital flow proxy are taken on a yearly basis to avoid seasonal fluctuations.

As mentioned in the introduction, our interest lies in the identification of Systemic Sudden Stops (or 3S), that is, Sudden Stops with an exogenous trigger. For this reason we require additionally that the detected Sudden Stop windows coincide with a period of skyrocketing *aggregate* spreads. The same methodology outlined above to detect large changes in capital flows is used for *aggregate* spreads to detect periods of capital market turmoil.[22]

We chose a sample of 110 countries, including 21 developed economies, and 89 developing countries for the period 1990–2004 (see the data appendix for details).[23] The set of countries and years in the sample is essentially restricted by availability of DLD data.

Two periods of financial turmoil for developing countries are detected in our sample: the neighborhood of the Tequila crisis (1994 to 1995) and the neighborhood of the East Asian–Russian Crisis (1998 to 1999). For developed countries, financial turmoil is detected for 1992, reflecting the

ERM crisis. During these three periods, a total of 77 3S crises are accounted for. A list of episodes is provided in appendix table A1. Our interest and the nature of the methodology we use to detect the 3S crises, for these periods of widespread financial turmoil, gathers the episodes "by construction," so that we look only at periods of systemic crises (large aggregate spreads). As a result all episodes are bunched, by definition, around systemic financial turmoil episodes.

However, it is worth asking whether bunching takes place when only large changes in capital flows are considered—that is, without imposing overlap with large fluctuations in *aggregate* spreads. Figure 7.1 displays the share of

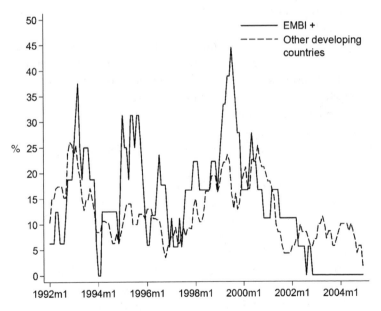

Figure 7.1
Bunching of Sudden Stops events: Emerging markets and other developing countries. For each group of countries, this figure displays the share of economies that experienced large changes in capital flows across time.

economies included in the EMBI+ index as well as other developing countries that experienced large changes in capital flows across time.[24] Bunching seems evident for EMBI+ countries, particularly around the Tequila crisis and the East Asian–Russian crisis (the two systemic events captured by large fluctuations in aggregate EMBI spreads), whereas there is no such clear bunching pattern for other developing countries, supporting the conjecture that EMs are particularly prone to contemporaneous, systemic events (our estimations will show that financial integration may be behind these results, as the probability of a 3S increases with financial integration in the early stages of integration). Given the heterogeneous nature of EMs in terms of their fiscal stance and other macroeconomic measures, it would be hard to argue that there was a common flaw in fundamentals driving these episodes, other than the fact that they are all EMs.[25] It is therefore clear to us that these episodes were not necessarily crises just waiting to happen—but rather, that they were triggered by an external event—although there may be factors that made some countries more prone to crisis, an issue that we raise earlier in this section and will discuss in the next section.

Another topic that is relevant to the hypothesis advanced in this study is whether Sudden Stop episodes have been associated with large RER depreciation—where large RER depreciation windows are defined along the same lines used to identify periods of large changes in capital flows. To this effect, we look at the share of 3S associated with large RER depreciation—that is, the number of 3S windows that overlap with large RER depreciation windows, relative to the number of 3S events. Thus 55 percent of 3S episodes can be linked to large RER depreciation, indicating that this large valuation element of balance sheet effects cannot be ignored.

Determinants of Sudden Stops: Empirical Analysis

Having defined Sudden Stops and examined some of their empirical characteristics, we now turn to a search for Sudden Stop determinants. The framework discussed above suggests balance-sheet factors that exacerbate an economy's vulnerability to Sudden Stops: the degree of domestic liability dollarization (both in the private and public sectors), as well as the sensitivity of the RER to capital flow reversals, which is related to the size of the supply of tradable goods relative to demand for tradable goods. Recall equation (6), which shows that the size of the increase in the RER depends on the percentage fall in the absorption of tradables needed to close the current account gap (CAD/Z).[26] Clearly, the less leveraged the absorption of tradable goods is, the smaller will be the effect on the RER. To show this, we rewrite CAD/Z as:

$$\frac{CAD}{Z} = \frac{Z - Y + S}{Z} = 1 - \frac{Y - S}{Z} = 1 - \omega, \tag{7}$$

where ω, defined as $\omega = (Y-S)/Z$, can be thought of as the unleveraged absorption of tradables. It is evident that the higher the supply of tradables (Y), the smaller will be financing from abroad (or leverage) of the absorption of tradables. Thus high values of $1 - \omega$ mean that a country relies less on its own financing of the absorption of tradables and is therefore more vulnerable to RER depreciation stemming from closure of the current account gap. Note that the denominator in (7) is the absorption of tradables and not GDP. This points to the fact that normalization of the current account deficit by the absorption of tradables may be more suitable than normalization by GDP when analyzing vulnerability to Sudden Stops.

In order to construct a measure of $1 - \omega$, the first component of balance-sheet effects tracking potential changes in RER, we need to obtain a value for the absorption of tradable goods (Z), which is composed of imports plus a fraction of the supply of tradable goods. We do this by using the sum of agriculture plus industrial output as a proxy for tradable output, that is, we exclude services from total output. Next, we obtain the fraction of tradable output consumed domestically by subtracting exports from tradable output and adding imports to the latter in order to get a measure of Z. Having computed values for Z, and using *CAD* data, we get values for $1 - \omega$ as in equation (7) (see the data appendix for details on definitions and sources for all the variables used in this section).

Our empirical strategy also highlights DLD, the second component of potential balance sheet effects, a phenomenon rarely considered in empirical studies of crises determination, with a few exceptions such as Arteta (2003), who explores the significance of liability dollarization in explaining the likelihood of a currency crisis. Interestingly, he finds no significant role for liability dollarization. This result is not incompatible with our findings below, given that we do not focus on currency crises, and, as stated earlier, the timing of currency crises may be quite different from that of Sudden Stops. Moreover, as it will become clear later in this chapter, our measure of dollarization is different.[27] A previous version of our study (Calvo, Izquierdo, and Mejía 2004) was the first to introduce the concept of DLD in determining the probability of a crisis. Here we conduct a much more comprehensive analysis by including a larger set of 110 countries for which DLD data are now available.[28]

For developed countries, DLD is defined as BIS reporting banks' local asset positions in foreign currency as a share of

GDP. Such data are not available for EMs, so we construct a proxy by adding up dollar deposits and domestic banks' foreign borrowing as a share of GDP. This measure should be a good proxy for liability dollarization, under the assumption that banks have a tendency to match the size of their assets and liabilities for each currency denomination.[29] Data on dollar deposits comes from Levy-Yeyati (2006), who builds on the dataset used by Honohan and Shi (2002). Data on bank foreign borrowing is obtained from IMF IFS (see the data appendix for a full description).

In contrast to measures of DLD previously used in the literature—such as scaling dollar credit as a share of total credit, or dollar deposits as a share of total deposits (as in Arteta 2003), we rely on liability dollarization as a share of GDP. This is particularly relevant to capture the fact that even though financial systems may not be heavily dollarized when considering the share of dollar liabilities in total liabilities, the size of the banking system may be sufficiently large that dollar liabilities as a share of GDP constitute a sizable burden to the economy in the event of large RER depreciation. For example, a region like East Asia, where the share of dollar liabilities in total liabilities is not large, comes at the same level as Latin America, where the share of dollar liabilities is large but the size of the banking system is small. One problem with this measure is that ideally one would like to capture only foreign-exchange denominated loans to nontradable sectors. This would not be a major problem if the share of foreign-exchange denominated loans to nontradables in total foreign-exchange denominated loans were about the same across countries. Preliminary evidence for a small subset of countries for which information is available suggests that there is a positive correlation between the degree of DLD and the share of dollar loans to nontradable sectors in total dollar loans, possibly reflecting the fact that nontradable sectors are a major client of domestic banking systems.[30] Another possibility that would validate our procedure is that in the short run most goods are de facto nontradable, as happened to Korea and Thailand in 1997 and also Brazil in 2002 when their export credit dried up, seriously impairing their ability to export even though large currency devaluation made exports extremely competitive.

Our estimation procedure uses as a benchmark a panel Probit model that approximates the probability of falling into a full-fledged 3S episode as a function of lagged values of $1 - \omega$ and DLD, controlling for a set of macroeconomic variables typically used in the literature on determinants of crises—which we describe later—and time effects using year dummies.[31] We use random effects to control for heterogeneity across panel members.[32]

In order to reduce endogeneity issues, and given that many of the variables used in our estimations come at an annual frequency, we switch to lagged yearly data.[33] We are particularly interested in lagged $1 - \omega$ because it proxies for the potential change in relative prices that could occur were the country to face an incipient Sudden Stop (recall the discussion in preceding section), something that would not be conveyed by contemporaneous $1 - \omega$ once the current account gap is closed and relative prices have adjusted.

A first set of regression results is presented in appendix table A2 (robustness checks, focusing on potential endogeneity issues between lagged $1 - \omega$ and the latent variable behind the construction of the Sudden Stop indicator, as well as estimations that focus only on developing countries are presented later in appendix tables A3 through A5). They indicate that both $1 - \omega$ and DLD are significant at the 1 percent level in most specifications. These results withstand the inclusion of a set of control variables typically used in the literature, including measures of financial integration such as the stock of FDI assets plus liabilities (as a share of GDP) and the stock of portfolio assets plus liabilities (as a share of GDP), terms of trade growth, the public sector balance and public external debt (all expressed as shares of GDP), the ratio of M2 to international reserves, as well as two different measures of exchange rate flexibility, and a developing country dummy (see columns 2 to 10 of appendix table A2).

Balance-sheet effects can be assessed by focusing on the interaction of ω and DLD, which is particularly amenable to Probit models given their nonlinear nature. We find that the effects of ω on the probability of a Sudden Stop crucially depend on the degree of DLD. Low values of ω (high leverage of CAD) imply a higher probability of Sudden Stop, but this is particularly so for dollarized economies. These effects are not only statistically significant, but economically significant as well. Consider, for example, the effects of varying ω on the probability of a Sudden Stop, keeping all other variables constant at their means, except for DLD, which could be low (5th percentile in our sample), average, or high (95th percentile). This is represented in figure 7.2 (panel a).[34] For small values of ω, there are substantial differences in the probability of a Sudden Stop depending on whether DLD is low or high. Take, for example, any two countries with a value of ω of 0.6 (the lowest measure of ω in our sample), and assume that the first country is highly dollarized (dotted line), whereas the second country is not (solid line). The probability of a Sudden Stop in the highly dollarized country exceeds that of the lowly dollarized country by about 17 percentage points. Now evaluate this difference for the same

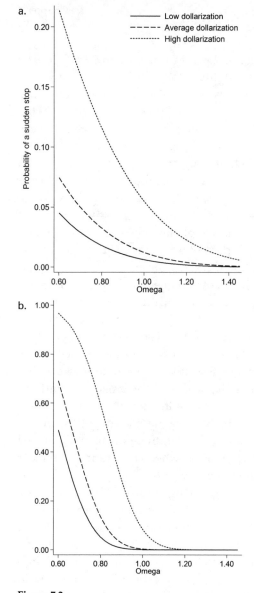

Figure 7.2
Probability of a Sudden Stop for different values of ω and domestic liability dollarization in the average country. (a) Not controlling for the endogeneity of ω; (b) controlling for the endogeneity of ω

two countries when ω is equal to 1 (i.e., when $CAD = 0$). The difference in the probability of a Sudden Stop is now only about 5 percentage points, about 30 percent of the difference at the lower ω level. The high nonlinearity described by the data implies that low ω and high dollarization can be a very dangerous cocktail, as potential balance sheet effects become highly relevant in determining the probability of a Sudden Stop. The effects of DLD on the probability of a Sudden Stop are particularly important for emerging markets. By the end of 1997—on the eve of the Russian crisis—61 percent of EMBI+ countries in our sample lay above the dollarization median, whereas 80 percent of developed countries lay below the dollarization median.[35]

We now turn to the set of variables used as controls in our regressions. We first focus on measures of financial integration based on data constructed by Lane and Milessi-Ferretti (2006). The first measure adds the absolute value of previous period FDI asset and liability stocks as a share of GDP, while the second measure does the same for portfolio stocks. A first pass suggests that both measures are broadly significant (mostly at the 5 percent level, although not in all specifications), indicating that higher integration reduces the probability of a Sudden Stop (however, these results will change for lower levels of integration when considering nonlinear effects, described in the next section).[36]

The coefficient accompanying terms-of-trade growth is negative as expected but not significant at the 5 percent level (appendix table A2, columns 5 through 10). Another variable of interest regarding Sudden Stops is the exchange rate regime. Two measures of exchange rate regime flexibility were used alternatively in the estimations presented in appendix table A2 (columns 7 through 10). These measures are those constructed by Levy-Yeyati and Sturzenegger

(2002), who classify the flexibility of exchange rate regimes based on exchange rate volatility, exchange-rate-changes volatility, and foreign reserves volatility.[37] The first, narrower measure classifies regimes into floating regimes, intermediate regimes, and fixed regimes, while the second measure extends this classification to five categories. This first pass suggests that both measures of exchange rate flexibility turn out not to be significant (although, as reported later, results are significant when focusing only on the developing country group and correcting for potential endogeneity issues). This finding may initially seem somewhat puzzling, but it can be explained by the fact that the loss of access to international credit is a real phenomenon with real effects such as output contraction, which, in principle, does not rely on the behavior of nominal variables. Indeed, the framework presented earlier in this chapter does not rely on any particular nominal setup to explain the change in relative prices following a Sudden Stop, which would materialize under both flexible and fixed exchange rate regimes. As a matter of fact, models that provide a full-fledged version of the effects of Sudden Stops on output such as Izquierdo (1999), Arellano and Mendoza (2002), and Calvo (2003) are concerned with real effects that are independent of nominal arrangements. Of course, this does not rule out very different short-term dynamics, which are likely to be dependent on nominal arrangements, as was evidenced by the very dissimilar behavior of several emerging economies after the Sudden Stop triggered by the Russian crisis of 1998. Even though most countries hit by Sudden Stops eventually experienced substantial real currency depreciation and output loss, the dynamics were very different for countries like Colombia, for example, which quickly depreciated its currency and withstood the real shock sooner, and Argentina, which took much longer to correct the resulting RER misalignment.[38]

The other macroeconomic variables that we added for control, including government balance as a share of GDP, and public sector external debt as a share of GDP (to capture effects in the same vein as our DLD variable), do not turn out to be significant across specifications (at least when not controlling for potential endogeneity of ω; we address this issue later on (see page 165)), although their coefficients show the expected signs. This is broadly consistent with other empirical work on the determinants of crises that do not find a strong relationship between these variables and the probability of crisis. The fact that ω as well as domestic DLD remain significant, while public external debt measures do not, suggests that valuation effects, coupled with the materialization of contingent liabilities resulting from public sector bailouts of private sector debts against the financial system may be key in explaining the likelihood of a Sudden Stop.[39]

A measure of the potential money and quasi-money liabilities that could run against international reserves, captured by the M2 to reserves ratio, was also added to the control group; again, although the coefficient accompanying this variable is positive, it is not statistically significant at the 10 percent level.

Finally, another vulnerability measure that has been associated with financial crises is the ratio of short-term debt to international reserves. Rodrik and Velasco (1999) use two versions of this variable as a determinant of financial crises for a group of emerging markets—separating short-term debt to foreign banks from other foreign short-term debt—and find these variables to be significant in explaining the probability of a financial crisis. In a separate exercise, we use the same (but updated) data source employed in their study (the International Institute of Finance's (IIF) database, comprising 31 emerging markets, substantially shrinking the sample size) to evaluate the impact of alternative measures of the the ratio of short-term debt to reserves on the probability of a Systemic Sudden Stop. For this relatively small subset of countries (compared to our sample of 110 countries used in other estimations), and controlling for balance-sheet effects, we do not find consistent evidence of either measure of short-term-debt-to-reserves-ratios being significant as a determinant of Systemic Sudden Stops.[40] This evidence is more in line with Frankel and Rose (1996), who find that short-term debt does not have an incidence on currency crises, and Eichengreen and Rose (1998), who find that short-term debt may decrease the probability of banking crises.

Robustness Checks
Addressing Endogeneity   Preliminary results indicate that a key driver of the balance-sheet effects affecting the probability of a Sudden Stop is the potential change in relative prices captured by $1 - \omega$. Yet, it is quite likely that this variable is endogenous with the latent variable behind Sudden Stops (capital flows) given their tight linkages through adjustments in the balance of payments, as well as unobserved and persistent characteristics common to both variables. Such would be the case of variables that proxy credibility or political factors. To tackle this potential endogeneity problem, we carried out a Rivers–Vuong test to the estimations previously presented in appendix table A2.[41] Based on the results of this test (see appendix table A3), we cannot reject the presence of endogeneity since the residuals obtained in the first stage of this method are significant in

Probit estimations.[42] A second element to consider is that this correction for endogeneity is done in the presence of random effects. Therefore, in order to assess the significance of all variables included in the estimations in the presence of endogeneity and random effects, we need to construct appropriate measures of the standard deviation of their coefficient estimators, as standard test statistics may no longer be valid (see the statistical appendix for a discussion). In order to do this, we rely on a nonparametric hierarchical two-step bootstrap methodology. Random effects introduce an intragroup correlation structure among observations. This is accounted for by first randomly sampling countries with replacements, and then randomly sampling without replacement within the sampled countries. According to Davison and Hinkley (1997), this procedure closely mimics the intragroup correlation structure of the data mentioned above (see the technical appendix for a detailed explanation). Confidence intervals are computed using the percentile method at the 1, 5, and 10 percent significance levels, based on 500 replications.

Including residuals of the first-stage regression in Probit estimations to control for endogeneity and using bootstrapped confidence intervals, we confirm that both $1 - \omega$ and domestic liability dollarization remain significant, this time at the 1 percent level in every specification. Results are reported in appendix table A3. Note, in particular, that the coefficient accompanying $1 - \omega$ increases substantially compared to results shown in appendix table A2, indicating that the relevance of $1 - \omega$ increases once controlling for endogeneity.[43] This can be seen graphically by replicating panel a of figure 7.2 with the new estimates, to show that for any given value of $1 - \omega$, the probability of a Sudden Stop increases compared to previous estimates that do not control for endogeneity (see panel b of figure 7.2). Also the nonlinearity of balance-sheet effects prevails.

After controlling for endogeneity and using bootstrapped confidence intervals, the public sector balance becomes significant at the 1 percent level in most specifications. Just one specification shows significance in terms of trade growth.

Using Only the Developing Country Sample In order to explore whether differences in potential balance-sheet effects remain a key explanatory variable within the developing-country group, and that they are not just capturing differences between developing and developed countries (despite the inclusion of a developing country dummy), we repeat our estimations, this time excluding developed countries. Results (already controlling for endogeneity and using bootstrapped confidence intervals) are shown in appendix table A4. Interestingly, we confirm the same results reached with the full dataset. Both $1 - \omega$ and DLD remain significant at the 1 percent level. The public balance is significant in all specifications (either at the 1 percent or 5 percent level), while terms of trade growth is not significant. But the key element to highlight here is that, for the group of developing countries, the exchange rate regime is significant across different definitions (three-way and five-way classification) in some specifications, in the sense that fixed exchange rate regimes are associated with a higher probability of a Sudden Stop.

Nonlinearities in Portfolio Integration In splitting the sample to include only developing countries, we found the portfolio integration coefficient changes sign and is significant at the 1 percent level in almost all specifications (see appendix table A4). This suggests that the probability of a

Sudden Stop *increases* with portfolio integration for this particular group, in stark contrast to results stemming from estimations including developed countries, for which the probability of a Sudden Stop *decreases* with financial integration. Bordo (2007) suggests that "financial revolutions" leading to *financial stability* depend on a set of "deep institutional factors" that countries can grow up to based on a learning process derived from experiencing financial crises. This would imply that while countries are integrating, they may be prone to financial crises, from which they can learn, so as to advance in their integration process until they become financially stable and therefore devoid of episodes such as Sudden Stops.[44]

Our findings regarding the switching sign of portfolio integration and the view stated above led us to explore the issue of nonlinearities in financial integration. To this effect, we included a quadratic term of our portfolio integration measure in our estimations for the full sample including both developing and developed countries (see appendix table A5).[45] The coefficient accompanying this quadratic term is negative and significant at the 1 percent level across specifications, while the linear term of portfolio integration is positive and significant at the 1 percent level. The inclusion of a quadratic term does not affect the significance at the 1 percent level of $1 - \omega$ or DLD across specifications, while the coefficient accompanying FDI integration is negative and now significant in most specifications. The public sector balance remains significant at either the 1 percent or 5 percent level. Terms-of-trade growth now comes up significant in a couple of specifications, a result that is consistent with the case made by Caballero and Panageas (2003) that in countries where commodities are relevant, a fall in commodity prices may be accompanied by a Sudden Stop, thus amplifying the original shock

Figure 7.3 depicts the relevance of nonlinearities in portfolio integration with respect to the probability of a Sudden Stop. Using estimations shown in column 4 of appendix table 5 (and keeping all other variables at their sample means), we find that countries with portfolio integration

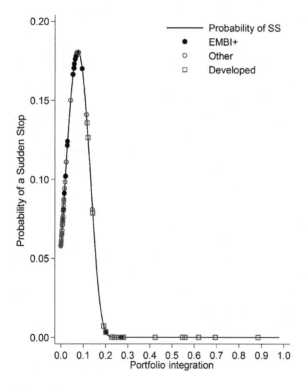

Figure 7.3
Probability of a Sudden Stop for different values of portfolio integration. The probability of a sudden stop is based on the estimation shown in column 4 of appendix table A5, with all other variables affecting the probability of a Sudden Stop evaluated at their sample means.

below 7.6 percent of GDP face an increasing probability of a Sudden Stop while, beyond this threshold, the probability of a Sudden Stop decreases with portfolio integration. Of particular interest is the placement of developed, EMBI+ and other developing countries in this figure. Notice that while most developed countries lie to the far right, and other developing countries mostly lie to the left, emerging markets that are part of the EMBI+ index are concentrated in the region where the probability of a Sudden Stop is highest. This is the group of countries that, despite the benefits of financial integration, may be facing the challenge of developing strong institutions that can ensure financial stability and reduce the probability of financial crises. An interesting result of this analysis is that it provides a rationale for a classification of emerging markets in accordance with their particular positioning in terms of integration and the likelihood of experiencing a Sudden Stop (a complete list of countries used in estimations and their position in terms of integration is provided in table A6).

Conclusions

In assessing the characteristics and determinants of large capital flow reversals of a systemic nature (suggestive of shocks to the supply of international funds) for a large set of developing and developed countries, we obtained a few key empirical findings that open up several areas of research:

• Systemic Sudden Stops tend to come hand in hand with large RER fluctuations, a key ingredient for balance-sheet effects.
• Sudden Stops seem to come in bunches, grouping together countries that are different in many respects, such

as fiscal stance, monetary and exchange rate arrangements. This particular type of bunching suggests that when analyzing Sudden Stops, careful consideration should be given to financial vulnerabilities to external shocks.

• A small supply of tradable goods (relative to the absorption of tradable goods), a proxy for large potential changes in the RER, and domestic liability dollarization, are key determinants of the probability of a Sudden Stop.

• The supply of tradable goods as well as the currency structure of balance sheets are in many respects the result of *domestic* policies. Countries may be tested by foreign creditors, but vulnerability to Sudden Stops is enhanced by domestic factors, such as tariff and competitiveness policies affecting the supply of tradable goods, and badly managed fiscal and monetary policies that result in domestic liability dollarization.

• The effect of balance-sheet factors on the probability of a Sudden Stop could be highly nonlinear. In particular, high leverage of tradables' absorption and high domestic liability dollarization could be a dangerous cocktail.

• The probability of a Sudden Stop initially increases with financial integration—departing from low levels of financial integration—but eventually decreases, and is virtually nil at high levels of integration. Emerging markets largely stand in a gray area in-between developed and other developing countries, where the probability of a Sudden Stop is the highest, suggesting that financial integration can be risky when not accompanied by the development of institutions that will support the use more sophisticated and credible financial instruments.

Although our work has established the empirical relevance of balance-sheet effects on the likelihood of Sudden

Stops, it does not cover two other topics that represent important extensions of the present line of research, namely the consequences of Sudden Stops and balance-sheet effects on economic growth, particularly in dollarized economies, as well as the role that international reserves could have in lowering the probability of Sudden Stops, by ameliorating the impact of balance-sheet effects .[46] We leave these topics for future research.

Appendix Tables

Table A1
Systemic Sudden Stop episodes

Country	Begins	Ends	Country	Begins	Ends
Developing countries			*Developing countries*		
Angola	1999m12	2001m3	Malawi	1997m12	1998m2
Argentina	1995m1	1995m12	Malaysia	1994m12	1995m9
Argentina	1999m5	1999m11	Mexico	1994m3	1995m11
Armenia	1997m12	1998m1	Moldova	1998m6	1999m8
Armenia	1998m9	2000m2	Mozambique	1995m3	1996m5
Azerbaijan	1997m9	1998m3	Nepal	1998m5	1999m7
Azerbaijan	1999m11	2001m4	Oman	1999m11	2001m4
Barbados	1999m1	1999m3	Pakistan	1995m9	1996m2
Belarus	1999m2	2000m1	Pakistan	1998m5	1999m1
Belize	1994m10	1995m9	Paraguay	1999m9	2001m5
Bolivia	1999m12	2000m10	Peru	1997m7	1998m2
Brazil	1995m1	1995m6	Peru	1999m2	1999m11
Brazil	1998m9	1999m8	Philippines	1995m5	1995m11
Bulgaria	1995m12	1996m10	Philippines	1997m5	1999m7
Cape Verde	1993m9	1994m7	Poland	1999m3	2000m5
Cape Verde	1997m3	1998m1	Sierra Leone	1998m1	1998m11

Table A1 (continued)

Country	Begins	Ends	Country	Begins	Ends
Developing countries			*Developing countries*		
Chile	1995m10	1996m8	Slovak Republic	1997m7	1998m4
Chile	1998m6	1999m6	Slovak Republic	1999m5	1999m9
Colombia	1997m12	2000m7	Slovenia	1998m6	1999m6
Costa Rica	1998m8	2000m8	Sri Lanka	1995m1	1996m8
Croatia	1998m9	1999m11	St. Kitts and Nevis	1993m7	1994m6
Dominican Republic	1994m3	1995m5	St. Vincent and the Grenadines	1995m2	1995m9
Ecuador	1995m5	1996m11	St. Vincent and the Grenadines	1999m3	1999m9
Ecuador	1999m7	2000m10	Suriname	1993m1	1994m5
El Salvador	1999m2	1999m10	Thailand	1996m12	1998m7
Estonia	1998m10	2000m2	Tonga	1998m4	1998m9
Guinea-Bissau	1999m1	1999m6	Turkey	1994m3	1995m1
Honduras	1995m10	1996m9	Turkey	1998m10	1999m9
Hong Kong, China	1998m7	1999m7	Uruguay	1999m3	1999m4
Indonesia	1997m12	1998m11	Uruguay	1999m12	2000m2
Indonesia	1999m12	2000m11	Yemen, Rep.	1994m6	1996m3
Jordan	1994m12	1995m5	Zimbabwe	1992m8	1994m10
Jordan	1998m10	1999m6	Zimbabwe	1997m6	1998m6
Korea, Rep.	1997m8	1998m11	Zimbabwe	1999m9	2001m5
Lao PDR	1997m7	1998m9	*Developed countries*		
Latvia	1999m4	1999m9	Austria	1992m2	1992m2
Lithuania	1999m5	2000m5	France	1992m1	1992m9
			Greece	1992m11	1993m7
			Portugal	1992m10	1993m9
			Spain	1992m4	1993m8
			Sweden	1992m1	1992m3

Table A2
Panel PROBIT. All countries—Dependent variable: Systemic Sudden Stop

	(1)	(2)	(3)	(4)	(5)	(6)	(7)	(8)	(9)	(10)
$1-\omega_{t-1}$	1.583***	1.339***	2.986***	2.403***	2.083***	2.570***	2.022***	2.010***	1.957***	1.656**
	(0.489)	(0.495)	(0.679)	(0.690)	(0.707)	(0.684)	(0.711)	(0.709)	(0.718)	(0.771)
DLD_{t-1}	1.005**	0.769*	2.109***	2.593***	2.760***	1.809**	1.977**	1.957**	2.063**	2.203***
	(0.419)	(0.421)	(0.726)	(0.792)	(0.808)	(0.707)	(0.786)	(0.784)	(0.808)	(0.825)
Developing dummy		0.859***	0.482	0.063	0.043	0.097	0.132	0.120	0.274	0.249
		(0.315)	(0.343)	(0.459)	(0.457)	(0.404)	(0.451)	(0.448)	(0.474)	(0.548)
FDI integration$_{t-1}$			-1.803***	-0.957*	-0.371	-1.280**	-0.840	-0.833	-0.806	-0.923
			(0.530)	(0.561)	(0.561)	(0.508)	(0.578)	(0.576)	(0.587)	(0.608)
Portfolio integration$_{t-1}$				-3.585*	-4.282**	-3.164*	-4.460**	-4.462**	-4.953**	-4.269*
				(2.033)	(2.045)	(1.846)	(2.150)	(2.142)	(2.220)	(2.299)
TOT growth$_t$					-0.846	-0.387	-0.585	-0.575	-0.542	-0.354
					(0.747)	(0.746)	(0.767)	(0.767)	(0.777)	(0.807)

Table A2 (continued)

	(1)	(2)	(3)	(4)	(5)	(6)	(7)	(8)	(9)	(10)
Public balance/ GDP $_{t-1}$						-0.006	-0.004	-0.004	-0.003	-0.003
						(0.004)	(0.005)	(0.005)	(0.005)	(0.005)
Ex. regime 3 $_{t-1}$							0.151			
							(0.116)			
Ex. regime 5 $_{t-1}$								0.092	0.098	0.097
								(0.074)	(0.075)	(0.077)
M2 over reserves $_{t-1}$									0.014	0.014
									(0.011)	(0.012)
Public external debt/ GDP $_{t-1}$										0.000
										(0.000)
Constant	-2.432***	-3.060***	-2.077***	-2.520***	-2.920***	-1.582***	-2.579***	-2.587***	-2.871***	-2.863***
	(0.197)	(0.339)	(0.359)	(0.500)	(0.520)	(0.413)	(0.546)	(0.555)	(0.611)	(0.669)

Table A2 (continued)

	(1)	(2)	(3)	(4)	(5)	(6)	(7)	(8)	(9)	(10)
Observations	1,081	1,081	927	921	903	849	796	796	795	661
Number of countries	110	110	94	94	90	84	83	83	83	72
McFadden adj R2	0.132	0.140	0.170	0.212	0.208	0.167	0.209	0.209	0.208	0.188
% Correctly predicted (PCP)	0.884	0.884	0.894	0.893	0.894	0.888	0.883	0.887	0.889	0.870
Adjusted PCP	-0.025	-0.025	0.125	0.116	0.103	0.095	0.079	0.109	0.129	0.122

Note: Standard errors in parentheses. All regressions include time dummies and random effects.
* significant at 10 percent, ** significant at 5 percent, *** significant at 1 percent.

Table A3

Panel PROBIT—Rivers—Young approach. All countries—Dependent variable: Systemic Sudden Stop

	(1)	(2)	(3)	(4)	(5)	(6)	(7)	(8)	(9)	(10)
Residuals$_t$	-3.443***	-3.306***	-8.097***	-7.991***	-8.948***	-8.638***	-7.977***	-7.940***	-7.798***	-12.345***
	[-8.86, -0.91]	[-7.84, -1.60]	[-15.99, -5.49]	[-17.63, -4.96]	[-20.11, -6.52]	[-16.47, -4.89]	[-16.81, -4.94]	[-16.25, -4.48]	[-16.24, -4.38]	[-27.00, -7.92]
$1 - \omega_{t-1}$	3.445***	3.210***	8.952***	8.403***	9.133***	9.101***	8.044***	8.010***	7.846***	12.13***
	[2.58, 8.33]	[2.47, 8.01]	[6.67, 18.75]	[6.41, 20.16]	[7.19, 23.38]	[7.18, 18.65]	[5.56, 18.90]	[5.58, 18.86]	[5.82, 18.22]	[8.75, 27.18]
DLD$_{t-1}$	1.946***	1.727***	4.193***	4.375***	4.507***	3.734***	4.214***	4.188***	4.174***	2.414***
	[1.07, 4.30]	[0.70, 3.92]	[3.42, 7.88]	[3.71, 8.40]	[4.10, 9.60]	[3.11, 7.86]	[3.49, 8.38]	[3.33, 8.86]	[3.35, 8.04]	[1.35, 5.60]
Developing dummy		0.651***	0.007	-0.367	-0.067	-0.035	-0.168	-0.187	-0.121	-0.264
		[0.03, 8.09]	[-0.50, 1.04]	[-1.32, 0.68]	[-0.91, 0.99]	[-0.77, 1.36]	[-1.07, 1.23]	[-1.19, 1.13]	[-1.16, 1.19]	[-1.44, 1.86]
FDI integration$_{t-1}$			-2.550***	-0.993***	-0.215	-1.714***	-1.717***	-1.683***	-1.666***	-2.421***
			[-5.39, -1.86]	[-3.81, -0.05]	[-1.73, 0.44]	[-4.65, -0.62]	[-5.03, -0.83]	[-5.50, -0.65]	[-6.14, -0.51]	[-7.46, -1.41]
Portfolio integration$_{t-1}$				-3.488***	-3.294*	-2.098	-3.138	-3.158	-3.349	-0.983
				[-9.72, -0.51]	[-8.42, -0.24]	[-6.10, 1.93]	[-8.73, 0.73]	[-9.28, 0.20]	[-9.80, 0.44]	[-6.08, 4.34]

Table A3 (continued)

	(1)	(2)	(3)	(4)	(5)	(6)	(7)	(8)	(9)	(10)
TOT growth$_t$					-1.607*	-1.221	-0.874	-0.871	-0.841	-0.700
					[-3.93, -0.28]	[-3.65, 0.26]	[-2.89, 0.63]	[-3.05, 0.83]	[-3.22, 0.77]	[-2.87, 1.07]
Public balance/ GDP$_{t-1}$						-0.079**	-0.093***	-0.093**	-0.092***	-0.100**
						[-0.26, -0.03]	[-3.86, -0.02]	[-0.30, -0.02]	[-3.43, -0.02]	[-1.25, -0.02]
Ex. regime$_{t-1}$ 3							0.165			
							[-0.02, 0.47]			
Ex. regime$_{t-1}$ 5								0.082	0.081	0.068
								[-0.04, 0.25]	[-0.05, 0.25]	[-0.10, 0.25]
M2 over reserves$_{t-1}$									0.006	-0.006
									[-0.02, 0.03]	[-0.04, 0.01]
Public external debt/ GDP$_{t-1}$										0.000
										[-0.00, 0.00]

Table A3 (continued)

	(1)	(2)	(3)	(4)	(5)	(6)	(7)	(8)	(9)	(10)
Constant	-2.773***	-3.245***	-2.257***	-2.959***	-3.837***	-2.300***	-3.215***	-3.150***	-3.228***	-2.871***
	[-4.73, -2.74]	[-11.95, -3.15]	[-11.32, -1.93]	[-6.29, -2.32]	[-14.18, -3.43]	[-13.96, -1.74]	[-17.02, -2.33]	[-19.38, -2.46]	[-14.51, -2.12]	[-15.98, -1.77]
Observations	1,071	1,071	919	913	897	843	792	792	791	658
Number of countries	110	110	94	94	90	84	83	83	83	72
McFadden adj R2	0.157	0.161	0.245	0.277	0.277	0.253	0.284	0.283	0.280	0.269
% Correctly predicted (PCP)	0.875	0.875	0.897	0.892	0.894	0.899	0.894	0.894	0.898	0.883
Adjusted PCP	-0.098	-0.098	0.152	0.116	0.112	0.190	0.168	0.168	0.198	0.214

Note: All regressions include time dummies and random effects. * significant at 10 percent, ** significant at 5 percent, *** significant at 1 percent, using bootstrapped confidence intervals constructed by the percentile method, shown in brackets.

Table A4
Panel PROBIT—Rivers—Voung approach. Developing countries—Dependent variable: Systemic Sudden Stop

	(1)	(2)	(3)	(4)	(5)	(6)	(7)	(8)	(9)
Residuals$_t$	-4.276***	-8.141***	-9.034***	-9.775***	-8.775***	-9.334***	-9.245***	-8.901***	-12.825***
	[-9.51, -1.51]	[-14.50, -5.19]	[-16.59, -5.95]	[-19.81, -6.32]	[-16.71, -4.82]	[-19.51, -6.09]	[-21.26, -5.65]	[-20.20, -4.67]	[-33.99, -7.83]
$1-\omega_{t-1}$	3.637***	9.262***	10.166***	10.756***	9.497***	9.838***	9.752***	9.359***	12.897***
	[2.55, 8.91]	[7.72, 17.12]	[8.18, 17.94]	[8.89, 20.07]	[7.51, 19.56]	[6.13, 23.15]	[7.57, 23.54]	[6.85, 24.44]	[9.74, 35.59]
DLD$_{t-1}$	2.378***	3.069***	2.629***	2.709***	2.522***	3.710***	3.666***	3.632***	2.836***
	[1.24, 5.46]	[2.19, 5.87]	[1.92, 5.61]	[1.95, 5.58]	[1.87, 5.51]	[3.01, 7.60]	[2.82, 8.30]	[3.00, 7.95]	[1.67, 7.91]
FDI integration$_{t-1}$		-0.575*	-1.558***	-1.398***	-1.692***	-2.074***	-2.030***	-1.923***	-1.281**
		[-1.76, -0.10]	[-3.85, -1.00]	[-3.61, -0.71]	[-5.06, -1.01]	[-8.63, -0.66]	[-7.18, -0.78]	[-8.00, -0.61]	[-5.12, -0.06]
Portfolio integration$_{t-1}$			8.604***	9.143***	8.644***	7.870***	7.681***	7.231***	3.638*
			[5.91, 17.41]	[6.41, 20.37]	[6.00, 18.30]	[1.02, 22.17]	[2.15, 22.91]	[0.04, 19.74]	[1.06, 11.09]
TOT growth$_t$				-0.819	-1.016	-0.925	-0.911	-0.853	-1.162
				[-2.79, 0.14]	[-3.30, 0.02]	[-3.67, 0.68]	[-3.80, 0.65]	[-3.63, 0.73]	[-4.34, 0.59]

Table A4 (continued)

	(1)	(2)	(3)	(4)	(5)	(6)	(7)	(8)	(9)
Public balance/ GDP$_{t-1}$					-0.065*** [-4.14, -0.02]	-0.105*** [-5.63, -0.02]	-0.103** [-1.25, -0.03]	-0.102** [-0.32, -0.03]	-0.197** [-6.10, -0.02]
Ex. regime$_{t-1}$ 3						0.283** [0.05, 0.79]			
Ex. regime$_{t-1}$ 5							0.160* [0.04, 0.42]	0.154* [0.04, 0.42]	0.069 [-0.08, 0.33]
M2 over reserves$_{t-1}$								0.018 [-0.01, 0.06]	0.015 [-0.02, 0.06]
Public external debt/ GDP$_{t-1}$									0.000 [-0.00, 0.00]

Table A4 (continued)

	(1)	(2)	(3)	(4)	(5)	(6)	(7)	(8)	(9)
Constant	-3.656*** [-6.84, -3.41]	-2.229*** [-3.72, -2.00]	-2.222*** [-3.59, -1.98]	-2.359*** [-4.08, -2.10]	-2.119*** [-3.67, -1.87]	-4.488*** [-10.17, -4.02]	-4.470*** [-21.75, -4.15]	-4.512*** [-17.78, -4.05]	-15.481*** [-421.58, -9.98]
Observations	833	681	675	660	606	566	566	565	540
Number of countries	89	73	73	70	64	63	63	63	60
Mcfadden R2	0.219	0.305	0.302	0.301	0.313	0.298	0.297	0.294	0.312
% Correctly predicted (PCP)	0.846	0.862	0.862	0.867	0.866	0.859	0.864	0.871	0.874
Adjusted PCP	-0.094	0.121	0.131	0.137	0.190	0.175	0.206	0.247	0.284

Note: All regressions include time dummies and random effects. * significant at 10 percent, ** significant at 5 percent, *** significant at 1 percent, using bootstrapped confidence intervals constructed by the percentile method, shown in brackets.

Table A5
Panel PROBIT—Rivers—Voung approach—Nonlinear portfolio integration. All countries—Dependent variable: Systemic Sudden Stop

	(1)	(2)	(3)	(4)	(5)	(6)	(7)
Residuals$_t$	-8.794***	-9.251***	-8.622***	-8.119***	-7.588***	-7.919***	-12.375***
	[-18.41, -5.94]	[-20.15, -6.25]	[-19.47, -5.46]	[-18.26, -5.29]	[-17.77, -5.00]	[-18.00, -4.19]	[-27.23, -7.36]
1- ω$_{t-1}$	9.316***	9.587***	8.717***	8.323***	7.864***	8.103***	12.166***
	[6.90, 21.92]	[7.04, 25.68]	[6.63, 20.70]	[6.12, 19.78]	[6.56, 18.67]	[6.86, 19.47]	[8.39, 31.65]
DLD$_{t-1}$	3.781***	4.032***	3.844***	3.798***	3.338***	3.743***	1.935***
	[3.17, 8.08]	[3.49, 8.89]	[3.13, 8.31]	[3.23, 7.71]	[2.75, 7.79]	[3.14, 7.95]	[1.06, 4.87]
Developing dummy	0.038	-0.026	-0.026	-0.186	0.189	-0.117	-0.178
	[-0.65, 0.96]	[-0.78, 1.01]	[-0.85, 1.07]	[-1.05, 0.99]	[-0.45, 1.59]	[-0.96, 1.06]	[-1.08, 7.01]
FDI integration$_{t-1}$	-0.554	0.132	-0.472	-1.413***	-1.350***	-1.338***	-2.046***
	[-2.18, 0.01]	[-1.33, 1.15]	[-2.58, 0.18]	[-7.43, -0.51]	[-5.38, -0.18]	[-5.87, -0.35]	[-7.44, -0.79]

Table A5 (continued)

	(1)	(2)	(3)	(4)	(5)	(6)	(7)
Portfolio integration$_{t-1}$	20.859***	20.795***	21.040***	17.769***	17.133***	17.472***	19.974***
	[11.69, 47.66]	[13.13, 53.40]	[11.91, 54.56]	[8.62, 47.02]	[7.86, 42.17]	[6.93, 41.65]	[10.27, 53.58]
(Portfolio integration$_{t-1}$)^2	-143.576***	-148.114***	-146.240***	-122.590***	-105.920***	-122.149***	-114.165***
	[-379.60, -75.90]	[-454.70, -97.40]	[-399.78, -61.78]	[-333.61, -71.34]	[-313.10, -59.21]	[-328.89, -60.36]	[-386.35, -62.73]
TOT growth$_t$		-1.646**	-1.741*	-0.850	-0.462	-0.811	-0.614
		[-5.08, -0.00]	[-4.13, -0.32]	[-3.28, 0.91]	[-2.83, 1.04]	[-3.00, 0.79]	[-3.01, 1.20]
Public balance/GDP$_{t-1}$			-0.091***	-0.094***	-0.076***	-0.092**	-0.098**
			[-1.63, -0.02]	[-3.82, -0.02]	[-5.54, -0.02]	[-0.36, -0.02]	[-0.38, -0.02]
Ex. regime$_{t-1}$ 3				0.154			
				[-0.00, 0.46]			
Ex. regime$_{t-1}$ 5					0.044	0.077	0.067
					[-0.07, 0.20]	[-0.03, 0.26]	[-0.09, 0.25]

Table A5 (continued)

	(1)	(2)	(3)	(4)	(5)	(6)	(7)
M2 over reserves$_{t-1}$						0.007	-0.002
						[-0.02, 0.03]	[-0.03, 0.02]
Public external debt/ GDP$_{t-1}$							0.000
							[-0.00, 0.00]
Constant	-3.738***	-4.215***	-3.979***	-3.442***	-2.936***	-3.483***	-3.228***
	[-8.07, -3.33]	[-15.31, -3.70]	[-24.24, -3.35]	[-16.35, -2.87]	[-12.67, -2.59]	[-14.53, -2.64]	[-15.78, -2.20]
Observations	913	897	843	792	792	791	658
Number of countries	94	90	84	83	83	83	72
McFadden adjR2	0.299	0.300	0.313	0.304	0.268	0.300	0.287
% Correctly predicted (PCP)	0.900	0.900	0.899	0.898	0.899	0.901	0.888
Adjusted PCP	0.188	0.159	0.190	0.198	0.208	0.228	0.245

Note: All regressions include time dummies and random effects. * significant at 10 percent, ** significant at 5 percent, *** significant at 1 percent, using bootstrapped confidence intervals constructed by the percentile method, shown in brackets.

Table A6
Portfolio integration results

Portfolio integration with positive effects on probability of Sudden Stop		Portfolio integration with negative effects on probability of Sudden Stop	
Country	Portfolio integration	Country	Portfolio integration
Azerbaijan	0.0%	Czech Republic	8.0%
Bolivia	0.0%	Mexico	9.5%
Cyprus	0.0%	Thailand	11.4%
Ethiopia	0.0%	Greece	11.6%
Kyrgyz Republic	0.0%	Japan	12.1%
Mozambique	0.0%	Chile	14.1%
Sudan	0.0%	Austria	14.2%
Zimbabwe	0.0%	Italy	19.2%
Haiti	0.0%	Malaysia	20.1%
Zambia	0.0%	New Zealand	20.1%
Nigeria*	0.0%	Spain	20.2%
Yemen, Rep.	0.0%	Portugal	22.8%
Uganda	0.0%	Norway	22.9%
Kuwait	0.1%	Germany	23.9%
Ecuador*	0.1%	United States	24.0%
Jamaica	0.1%	Denmark	24.9%
Paraguay	0.1%	South Africa	26.8%
Angola	0.1%	France	27.2%
Belarus	0.1%	Australia	28.1%
Lao PDR	0.1%	Canada	42.4%
Armenia	0.2%	Sweden	54.8%
Georgia	0.2%	Belgium	55.9%
Kenya	0.3%	Finland	62.1%
El Salvador	0.4%	United Kingdom	69.5%

Table A6 (continued)

Portfolio integration with positive effects on probability of Sudden Stop		Portfolio integration with negative effects on probability of Sudden Stop	
Country	Portfolio integration	Country	Portfolio integration
Trinidad and Tobago	0.4%	Netherlands	88.5%
Romania	0.4%	Hong Kong, China	133.7%
Malawi	0.5%	Switzerland	149.7%
Uruguay	0.6%		
Costa Rica	0.6%		
Dominican Republic	0.7%		
Moldova	0.7%		
Lithuania	0.8%		
Sri Lanka	0.8%		
Bulgaria*	0.8%		
Oman	0.9%		
Jordan	1.0%		
Ukraine*	1.1%		
Kazakhstan	1.2%		
Slovenia	1.3%		
Latvia	1.4%		
Colombia*	1.5%		
Pakistan	1.7%		
Mauritius	1.8%		
Poland*	2.0%		
Croatia	2.4%		
Egypt, Arab Rep.*	2.9%		
Turkey*	3.0%		
Indonesia	4.3%		

Table A6 (continued)

Portfolio integration with positive effects on probability of Sudden Stop		Portfolio integration with negative effects on probability of Sudden Stop	
Country	Portfolio integration	Country	Portfolio integration
Peru*	5.4%		
Venezuela, RB*	5.7%		
Korea, Rep.*	6.0%		
Brazil*	6.4%		
Argentina*	6.7%		
Philippines*	7.2%		
Hungary	7.4%		
Estonia	7.6%		

Note: * Countries tracked by JPMorgan's EMBI+. Countries in which portfolio integration affects positively (negatively) the probability of sudden stop are those whose average portfolio integration is below (above) 7.6 percent. This cutoff value was calculated as the level of portfolio integration that maximizes the probability of sudden stop: $-\alpha/2\beta$, where α is the estimated coefficient of the linear term of portfolio integration and β is the estimated coefficient of the quadratic term of portfolio integration. This cutoff value was calculated using equation 4 of appendix table A5. The list shows the average of portfolio integration for observations that were included in the estimation of equation 4. If instead averages were computed for all available data of portfolio integration from 1990 to 2004, Czech Republic would move to the group of countries in which portfolio integration affects positively the probability of a Sudden Stop. Iceland, Israel, Bahrain, Libya, United Arab Emirates, Ireland, and Luxemburg would be listed in the group in which portfolio integration affects negatively the probability of a Sudden Stop. The rest of countries in Lane and Millesi-Ferreti's (2006) dataset not mentioned in this note or in the table would be listed in the group in which portfolio integration affects positively the probability of a Sudden Stop.

Data Appendix

Our sample of 110 countries is divided into 21 developed economies and 89 developing economies. Our choice of developed countries is dictated by OECD membership, and it includes Australia, Canada, Denmark, Finland, France, Germany, Italy, Japan, Netherlands, New Zealand, Norway, Portugal, Spain, Sweden, Switzerland, United Kingdom, and United States. The list of developing countries includes Angola, Antigua and Barbuda, Argentina, Armenia, Azerbaijan, Bangladesh, Barbados, Belarus, Belize, Bolivia, Brazil, Bulgaria, Cape Verde, Chile, Colombia, Costa Rica, Croatia, Cyprus, Czech Republic, Dominica, Dominican Republic, Ecuador, Egypt Arab Rep., El Salvador, Estonia, Ethiopia, Fiji, Georgia, Ghana, Grenada, Guatemala, Guinea-Bissau, Haiti, Honduras, Hong Kong (China), Hungary, Indonesia, Jamaica, Jordan, Kazakhstan, Kenya, Korea Rep., Kuwait, Kyrgyz Republic, Lao PDR, Latvia, Lithuania, Malawi, Malaysia, Maldives, Mauritius, Mexico, Moldova, Mongolia, Morocco, Mozambique, Nepal, Nicaragua, Nigeria, Oman, Pakistan, Papua New Guinea, Paraguay, Peru, Philippines, Poland, Romania, Rwanda, Sierra Leone, Slovak Republic, Slovenia, South Africa, Sri Lanka, St. Kitts and Nevis, St. Lucia, St. Vincent and the Grenadines, Sudan, Suriname, Thailand, Tonga, Trinidad and Tobago, Turkey, Uganda, Ukraine, Uruguay, Venezuela RB, Yemen Rep., Zambia, and Zimbabwe. Data are collected on an annual basis unless otherwise stated. Data span from 1992 to 2004.

Variable	Definitions and sources
Capital flows proxy	A monthly proxy is obtained by netting out changes in international reserves from the trade balance. Based on this proxy, 12-month cumulative annual flows are constructed for each month. Annual differences of the latter are then used to measure capital account changes. All figures are expressed in 2000 US dollars. Source: IMF IFS.
Aggregate sovereign bond Spread index	EMBI for EMs (source: J.P. Morgan), Euro-area government bond spread index for Euro-area countries (source: Merrill Lynch), G7 government bond spread index for all remaining developed countries (source: Merrill Lynch).
Systemic Sudden Stop (3S) dummy	We define a 3S dummy as a capital-flow window that overlaps at any point in time with an aggregate-spread window. A capital-flow window contains a large fall in the capital flows proxy exceeding two standard deviations from its mean (that starts when the fall in the capital flows proxy exceeds one standard deviation, and ends when it is smaller than one standard deviation). Capital-flow windows less than 6 months apart were considered as part of the same event. Aggregate-spread windows contain those years in which a spike in the corresponding bond spread index exceeds two standard deviations from its mean (it starts when I the spread exceeds one standard deviation, and ends when it is smaller than one standard deviation). All calculations were performed at a monthly frequency and then transformed to annual frequency for Probit estimation.
Absorption of tradable goods (Z)	Imports plus tradable output domestically consumed, proxied by the sum of agricultural and industrial output minus exports. More specifically, we construct the share of tradable output in total output as the ratio of agriculture plus industrial output to total GDP at constant prices. Next, we multiply this share by total dollar GDP to obtain the dollar value of tradable output. We do this in order to avoid excessive fluctuations in output composition due to valuation effects that are present in sectoral data at current prices. Source: World Bank, World Development Indicators.

Variable	Definitions and sources
CAD	Current account deficit. Source: IMF's World Economic Outlook (WEO) database.
Domestic liability dollarization (DLD)	For developed economies: BIS reporting banks' local asset positions in foreign currency as a share of GDP (since data for Australia and New Zealand is not available from this source, we used data from their respective Central Banks). For developing economies: dollar deposits obtained from Levy-Yeyati (2006) (based on Honohan and Shi (2002)) plus bank foreign borrowing (IMFIFS banking institutions line 26c) as a share of GDP.
FDI integration	FDI Liabilities plus FDI Assets over GDP. Source: Lane and Millesi-Ferreti (2006)
Portfolio integration	Portfolio Liabilities plus Portfolio Assets over GDP. Source: Lane and Millesi-Ferreti (2006)
External public debt	Data on external public debt were obtained from IMF IFS (for some developing countries, data was obtained from World Bank's Global Development Finance database (GDF).
TOT growth	Annual rate of change of terms of trade on goods and services. Source : IMF's WEO (April 2006).
Ex. regime 3	3-way exchange regime classification: 1 = float; 2 = intermediate (dirty, dirty/crawling peg); 3 = fix. Source: Levy-Yeyati and Sturzenegger (2002)
Ex. regime 5	5-way exchange regime classification: 1 = inconclusive; 2 = float; 3 = dirty; 4 = dirty/crawling peg; 5 = fix. Source: Levy-Yeyati and Sturzenegger (2002)
GDP	Gross domestic product. Source: IMF's WEO database.
M2	Money plus quasi-money. Source IMF IFS.
Public balance	General government balance to GDP ratio. Source: IMF's WEO database.
Large RER depreciation dummy	Dummy variable that takes the value of 1 when a large rise on RER (vis-à-vis US dollar) occurs and 0, otherwise. We define a rise in the RER (i.e., real depreciation of the currency) to be large when it exceeds two standard deviations above the sample mean prevailing before the rise.

Variable	Definitions and sources
Reserves	International Reserves. Source: IMF IFS
Short-term debt to foreign banks and other short-term debt due to foreigners	Source: International Institute of Finance Database. Short-term debt to foreign banks (series D353). Other short-term debt was obtained by subtracting series D353 from series D204 (total short-term debt).

Technical Appendix: Inference with Random-Effects Probits under Endogeneity

Walter Sosa Escudero[1]

This note is concerned with estimation and inference in a random effects Probit specification allowing for possibly endogenous explanatory variables. The standard random effects Probit model with exogenous explanatory variables is

$$y_{it}^* = x_{it}'\beta + \mu_i + \varepsilon_{it}, \qquad i = 1, 2, \ldots, n; \ t = 1, 2, \ldots, T,$$

where x_{it} is a k vector of exogenous explanatory variables, β is a k vector of coefficients, μ_i is IN(0, σ_μ^2), and ε_{it} is IN(0, σ_ε^2). The observed binary random variable y_{it} is related to the model through

$$y_{it} = 1[y_{it}^* > 0].$$

Maximum likelihood estimation (MLE) of this model is extensively studied in Heckman (1981) and reviewed in Hsiao (2003). The likelihood function for this problem is given by

$$L = \prod_{i=1}^{N} \int_{-\infty}^{+\infty} \prod_{t=1}^{T} \Phi \left\{ \left[(x_{it}'\beta/\sigma_\varepsilon) + \tilde{\mu}_i \left(\frac{\rho}{1-\rho} \right)^{1/2} \right] [2y_{it} - 1] \right\} f(\tilde{\mu}_i) d\tilde{\mu}_i,$$

where $\rho = \sigma_\mu^2 / \sigma_\varepsilon^2$. The evaluation of the integral in the previous expression is not trivial and it is usually carried out through Hermite integration or simulation.

Guilkey and Murphy (1993) conducted an extensive Monte Carlo experiment to study the small sample behavior of alternative estimation strategies of the random effects Probit model. The most important results that are relevant for this study are summarized below:

1. Standard Probit and MLE of the random effects Probit provide consistent estimation of β.
2. The standard Probit estimator of the standard errors of the estimators is markedly downward biased, leading to incorrect inferences, in the sense of suggesting significant coefficients when in fact they are not.
3. The random effects MLE based estimator provides more accurate estimators of the standard errors but the gain in performance is relatively mild when compared to that of the standard Probit.
4. For small individual observations (N around 25), the numerical accuracy problems involved in the evaluation of the integral shown above severely affect the performance of the procedure, invalidating the use of standard asymptotic approximations.

The possibility of allowing for endogenous explanatory variables has been studied in the context of the standard Probit model:

$$y_j^* = z_j \gamma + x_j' \beta + u_j, \qquad j = 1, 2, \ldots, J,$$

where u_j is $IN(0, \sigma_u^2)$; x_j, β, and y_j^* are defined as in the previous model; and z_j is a possibly endogenous explanatory variable. Rivers and Vuong (1988) provided a simple estimation strategy for the case where

$$z_j = \tilde{x}_j \delta + v_j,$$

and (u_j, v_j) have a bivariate normal distribution independent of $\tilde{x}_j$. $\tilde{x}_j$ is a vector of exogenous explanatory variables in the reduced-form model for z_j, which in this context is endogenous if and only if u_j and v_j are correlated. Rivers and Vuong (1988) propose a consistent estimation[2] based on a two-step approach:

• Step 1: Run the OLS regression of z_j on $\tilde{x}_j$ and save residuals $\hat{v}_j$.
• Step 2: Run a standard Probit regression of y_j on x_j, z_j and $\hat{v}_j$.

Details of the procedure can be checked in the original reference and in Wooldridge (2002). The main intuition behind the result comes from the fact that under bivariate normality of u and v, we can write $u_j = \theta v_j + \eta_j$, where η_j is independent of $\tilde{x}_j$ and v_j; then, replace it in the definition of y_j^*:

$$y_j^* = z_j \gamma + x_j' \beta + \theta v_j + \eta_j.$$

If v_j were observable, consistent estimation could proceed by a standard Probit regression of y_j on z_j, x_j and v_j, since, by construction, all explanatory variables are exogenous with respect to η_j. The first stage of the Rivers–Vuong procedure replaces v_j by a consistent estimate obtained from OLS regression in a first stage.

The performance of the Rivers and Vuong (1988) procedure in the context of the random effects specification has not been explored, and though it deserves a more detailed exploration than the one offered here, some insights can be discussed. A simple extension in the panel context, as described in the first equation of this appendix, is to allow for endogenous explanatory variables by allowing for correlation between the observation specific error term of the index model (ε_{it}) and the error term of the reduced form of the possibly endogenous explanatory variable (v_{it}). In this context, the index model can be written as

$$y_{it}^* = z_{it}\gamma + x_{it}'\beta + \theta v_{it} + \mu_i + \eta_{it},$$

and, again, if v_{it} were observable, the model should be unaltered albeit for some redefinition of relevant parameters. In this case, the Rivers–Vuong procedure is replacing an exogenous explanatory variable (v_{it}) with a consistent estimate obtained from a first-stage regression.

An important problem is how to perform reliable inference with the proposed method. As discussed previously, Guilkey and Murphy (1993) suggest that the numerical accuracy problem related to the evaluation of the likelihood function of the random effects Probit makes asymptotic approximations very unreliable. A natural possibility is to consider a bootstrap approach. The nature of such procedure in this context is complicated due to the fact that, by construction, observations are not independent due to the presence of a random effect. In this appendix we follow Davison and Hinkley (1997) and use a nonparametric hierarchical two-step bootstrap strategy, where in a first stage, individuals are randomly sampled with replacements, and, in a second stage, observations are randomly sampled without replacement within the individuals sampled in the first stage. According to Davison and Hinkley (1997, pp. 100–102), this procedure closely mimics the intragroup correlation structure of the data, due to the presence of the individual random effect.

Notes

1. Universidad de San Andrés, Victoria, Argentina. Email: wsosa@udesa.edu.ar. Martin Cicowiez provided excellent computing support.

2. As it is usual in binary choice index models, not all the parameters are identified; hence appropriate normalizations must be adopted. See Rivers and Vuong (1988) for details on this subject.

References

Davison, A., and D. Hinkley. 1997. *Bootstrap Methods and Their Applications*. Cambridge, UK: Cambridge University Press.

Guilkey, D., and J. Murphy. 1993. Estimation and testing in the random effects Probit Model. *Journal of Econometrics* 59: 301–17.

Heckman, J. 1981. Statistical models for discrete panel data. In C. Manksi and D. McFadden, eds., *Structural Analysis of Discrete Data with Econometric Applications*. Cambridge: MIT Press.

Hsiao, C. 2003. *Analysis of Panel Data*, 2nd ed. Cambridge, UK: Cambridge University Press.

Rivers, D., and Q. Vuong. 1988. Limited information estimators and exogeneity tests for simultaneous Probit models. *Journal of Econometrics* 39: 347–66.

Wooldridge, J. 2002. *Econometric Analysis of Cross Section and Panel Data*. Cambridge: MIT Press.

Notes

Preface

1. I must confess, however, that part of the inspiration for the title also came from one of the great books by Gabriel García Márquez: *El Amor en los Tiempos del Cólera* (translated into English as *Love in the Time of Cholera*).

2. This is in line with my two Ohlin lectures entitled "Liquidity Illusions and Delusions" (September 25, 2012) and "Sudden Stop, Fall of Output and Employment, and Over-Indebtedness" (September 26, 2012).

3. Paradigmatic examples in this regard are the Russian 1998 and Lehman 2008 crises, discussed in chapter 1.

Introduction

1. Liquidity will be more fully defined and treated in chapter 2.

2. To be fair, I should say that I ran into the PTM by myself before reading Keynes's paragraph where he presents it as a conjecture (is Plato right, after all?).

3. Some of the results obtained in this context could be replicated in models subject to important nonlinearities that display equilibrium uniqueness (e.g., see Mendoza 2010; Brunnermeier and Sannikov 2014). This will be further discussed in chapter 3.

4. It is worth noting that despite all the sophistication displayed by rational-expectations models, most modern textbooks have not dumped Hicks's (1937) IS/LM model—the archetypical ad hoc macro model!

5. See Teulings and Baldwin (2014) for essays on the phenomenon of "secular stagnation" as being partly due to a deterioration of the financial sector. Barclays (2015) argues that means of exchange relevant for global trade and finance (called Safe Assets) have not recovered from the Lehman crisis.

Chapter 1

1. Sudden Stop became a popular concept in the context of EMs. It refers to a period in which external capital inflows show a large and largely unexpected fall; see Izquierdo (2013) and part II of this book. Sudden Stop is also applied to domestic credit *flows*, a phenomenon that I will call "domestic credit Sudden Stop."

2. Mexico's fiscal deficit as a share of GDP was only 0.6 percent in 1994 according to the WEO, but it was considerably higher if the potential deficit of a domestic development bank is taken into account. Interestingly, Mexico's fiscal deficit reached 4 and 5 percent of GDP in 1995 and 1996, respectively, despite a quick output recovery. This illustrates the possibility that fiscal deficits may partly be a *consequence* of financial crisis, not just a cause.

3. The spread is relative to comparable US public sector debt instruments.

4. In chapter 6, Sudden Stops that coincide with a sharp rise of the average EMBI are called "systemic."

5. New models containing sharp nonlinearities can account for this kind of phenomena, but they were not part of the macroeconomist's toolkit. See the end of chapter 3.

6. These issues are further discussed in chapter 7.

7. See Brunnermeier (2009) for an excellent narrative on this crisis.

8. The TED spread is the difference between interbank loan rate (measured by the LIBOR) and interest rate on short-term US Treasury bills.

9. This has to be taken with a grain of salt because FDI includes retained earnings from past foreign investment, and earnings sharply increased in some EMs (e.g., South America), thanks to a boom in commodity prices.

10. QE had already been tried in Japan in the 1990s with limited success.

11. Neutrality of interest rate policy is in accord with the conventional wisdom. However, agency problems that highlight the importance of credit collateral point to the possibility that neutrality does not hold. I would even

conjecture that interest rate policy may be highly nonneutral in EMs whose institutions are weak.

Chapter 2

1. I am deeply indebted to Sara Calvo, Enrique Mendoza, and Carmen Reinhart for their insightful and comprehensive comments. However, I am solely responsible for errors and opinions.

2. Hicks's quotation at the beginning of this chapter, though, shows that our predecessors' best minds were keenly aware of the possibly serious fragilities underlying a monetary economy. Unfortunately, these issues have proved to be too subtle for textbook writers, who have left their readers blissfully ignorant about major liquidity disruptions until the Lehman episode.

3. Models where money is just a veil over the *real* sector offer a deep insight about the nature of "money." However, as will become apparent in the ensuing discussion, this insight applies to a special kind of money under special circumstances, and may have blindsided economists about the vulnerabilities associated with 'money' in actual monetary economies.

4. "Basket of goods" is an avowedly imprecise expression. It is intended to convey the notion that the pledgeable share of an asset can be readily employed to acquire a wide variety of goods or assets.

5. The following example follows on the footsteps of the seminal paper by Diamond and Dybvig (1983).

6. This would not hold true if the central bank pegged the exchange rate to another currency, a usual practice in EMs (see Calvo and Reinhart 2002). But, even in that case, the central bank's obligation is typically to exchange domestic currency for foreign currency, which does not take domestic currency outside the extrinsically liquid assets' circle.

7. This statement may be questioned because the Fed could resort to the Treasury for additional resources. However, this is doubtful in the case of the US because public debt and fiscal deficit are large, especially if one takes into account the present discounted value of unfunded liabilities (e.g., Medicare).

8. Actually Hahn (1965) shows that, in standard general equilibrium models, barter equilibriums, where money's output value is nil, cannot be ruled out. This poses a fundamental challenge to monetary theory, which macroeconomists have thoroughly disregarded (see Calvo 2012a).

9. One is tempted to quip that perhaps "In God We Trust," written on the back of US dollar bills, should be modified into "In God *and Sticky Prices* We Trust."

10. This is partly due to the fact that despite the existence of new instruments to palliate the consequences of liquidity crunch (e.g., the IMF Flexible Credit Line), the rules adopted by the IFIs are unclear, and EM policy makers are afraid to fall prey of the IFI officer in charge.

11. The strength of DM currencies has permitted DMs to utilize monetary policy as a fiscal revenue instrument. For example, the Fed has accumulated large amounts of "toxic assets," while the European Central Bank is starting to buy public debt from peripheral members of the euro zone, whose "ability to pay" is highly debatable.

12. The role of credit in exacerbating the impact of financial crisis on the real sector has been recently been emphasized by Mendoza (2010), Brunnermeier and Schnabel (2015), and Jordà et al. (2015).

13. Notice that in the United States, price level deflation was staved off, but it could be argued that debt deflation was not prevented because monetary policy was not strong enough to keep *nominal* real estate prices from collapsing.

14. This outcome can easily be shown in the context of the IS/LM model with predetermined prices.

15. For a growth model bearing out this type of outcome, see chapter 5.

16. These concepts are akin to intrinsic and extrinsic liquidity discussed above, but they are not identical. I hope this causes no confusion. I keep this terminology because we used it in an already published paper (see Calvo, Coricelli, and Ottonello 2013; see also chapter 6).

17. This way of formalizing central bank interest rates was originally suggested in Calvo and Végh (1995). The present version would strictly hold if, say, Treasury bills are the only form of money and the central bank sets its interest rate, here denoted i^m. This will be further discussed in chapter 3.

18. This issue is highlighted in Mendoza, Quadrini, and Rios-Rull (2009) as a relevant factor behind the global imbalance phenomenon.

19. A question that I do not think has yet been fully answered is why, relative to the subprime, the dot-com crisis had minor and short-lived deleterious effects. My conjecture is that shadow banks were less important in 2001 than in 2007. However, the dot-com crisis could have set the ground for the 2008 blowout by inducing the Fed to implement low-interest rates for a

considerable period of time, which might have led to a strong surge of shadow banking (see Calvo 2012b and chapter 6 below). Another conjecture is that the real estate boom was financed by credit while the dot-com bubble was mostly equity financed; see Turner (2015).

20. During the hyperinflation episode in Argentina in 1989, price indexation and high volatility were rampant. As a result many stores closed and posted intriguing notices reading "closed for *lack* of prices." They should have said "lack of externally liquid assets." Even the dollar failed as a unit of account!

Chapter 3

1. Actually Patinkin (1949) is a forerunner. His study shows that the classical separation between the theory of value and monetary theory is inconsistent with utility maximization under budget constraint.

2. A few "currency substitution" models assume that more than one type of money circulates in the economy. Currency substitution models belong to the family of models where liquidity issues play a significant role, see, for example, Calvo and Végh in Calvo (1996, ch. 8). This issue was discussed in chapter 2.

3. See Calvo (2012 a) for further discussion.

4. See Obstfeld and Rogoff (1983, 1986). These studies show that, in addition to converging equilibrium solutions, there may be nonconverging solutions exhibiting hyperinflation. The papers also discuss assumptions that rule out hyperinflation. However, Calvo (2012a) argues that these models' rule barter equilibriums by assumption.

5. See Obstfeld (1986).

6. Nonlinear models could be free from this criticism. See discussion at the end of this chapter.

7. This does not call for throwing these models into the wastebasket. However, to become relevant these models must add critical aspects that have been ignored in pre-crisis models—in particular, capital market frictions. Fortunately, the current literature is moving in that direction. See the end of this chapter for some discussion.

8. However, the FTPL would still apply if κ is state contingent but independent of monetary policy, and market agents include that in formulating their expectations—a highly debatable assumption given the typical disarray and confusion involved in debt default negotiations.

9. Capital flight in EMs is equivalent to a *fall* (not a rise) in coefficient θ attached to EM public debt instruments. Thus, if fiscal policy stays put, the price level will rise. As pointed out in previous chapters, the latter causes debt deflation type of financial stress because EMs often suffer from liability dollarization or original sin (see Eichengreen et al. 2005), a situation in which debt is denominated in terms of foreign currency (dollar or euro, mostly). This may thus prompt fiscal tightening, a policy often called for in IMF programs, making fiscal policy passive.

10. Note that $q \to \infty$ as $\theta \to 1$, which implies that liquidity from land holding $\theta qk \to \infty$. Under normal conditions in which the demand for liquidity is finite, money holding will eventually hit 0, a corner solution. Corner solutions will be explored in chapter 5.

11. However, the liquidity deflation phenomenon discussed in chapter 2 makes the fall in θ possible and even relevant if central banks follow an aggressive expansion of money supply, as in the QE experiments these days.

12. See, for example, Dabús (2008) and references cited there.

13. This assumption is akin to the one raised in the Ohlin–Keynes debate about the rate of interest (see Davidson 1965; Tsiang 1980).

14. It is worth noting that equilibrium multiplicity with money in the production function might hold in flexible-prices models, even though money supply is constant over time (see Calvo 1979).

15. See Calvo (2012b) for an alternative proof of this proposition.

16. This becomes evident in their discussion of the Lehman crisis, which relies on assuming some form of exogenous liquidity crunch, equivalent to a sudden exogenous decline in θ in the above model (e.g., see the epilogue in Holmström and Tirole 2011, p. 227).

17. See, for instance, Mendoza (2010), Korinek and Mendoza (2013), Christiano and Ikeda (2013), and Brunnermeier and Sannikov (2014). For further discussion about the macro impact of collateral constraints, see Kiyotaki and Moore (1997) and Geanakoplos (2010).

18. Compare this with the staggered prices model in which at *every point in time* a negligible number of individuals are hit by a shock that may lead them to behave in a discontinuous manner. This does not result in discontinuity at the macro level.

19. Enrique Mendoza and his collaborators are exploring this issue for an NSF project (personal conversation).

Chapter 4

1. See Woodford (2003).

2. See, for example, Calvo and Végh (1995).

3. The relevance of liquidity of public debt instruments is also highlighted in nonmonetary contexts in Woodford (1990) and Hölmstrom and Tirole (2011), for example.

4. Canzoneri and Diba (2005) study a similar model but do not draw attention to this implication.

5. In a related model Canzoneri et al. (2009) suggest this result by means of numerical simulations.

6. Cash-in-advance is the standard assumption in this literature, but I chose the present form to make results directly comparable with those in Calvo (1983).

7. Parameter θ is unrelated to the liquidity coefficient in chapter 3.

8. Note that $\theta > 1$ implies that the interest rate on liquid bonds increases faster than inflation. Thus, higher inflation induces a higher demand for liquid bonds. Contrast this with the conventional case in which an increase in the rate of interest controlled by the monetary authority raises the *opportunity cost of money* (the only liquid asset contemplated in conventional models). Thus $\theta > 1$ is formally equivalent to making the demand for money an *increasing* function of the rate of interest in conventional models, a situation that, as can easily be verified, gives rise to a continuum of converging equilibrium paths.

9. This assumption ensures existence of steady state with $\pi = 0$.

10. In Calvo (1983) the proof relies on a cross-product condition for characteristic roots, in which θ would enter. But it looks to me now (more than 30 years later!) that the condition was not necessary for the proof.

11. See Woodford (2009).

Chapter 5

1. I am grateful to Fabrizio Coricelli and Carmen Reinhart for useful comments.

2. In Stockman (1981), the Finance Motive is not attributed to Keynes or post-Keynesians like Davidson (1965). However, Stockman cannot be

blamed for the omission because the Finance Motive was ignored in mainstream macroeconomics. In fact I discovered it almost by chance shortly before writing this book!

3. More precisely, $f(x)$ is increasing, strictly convex, continuously differentiable on the set of nonnegative real numbers, and satisfies Inada conditions.

4. For economy of notation, I will skip *time* subscripts unless they are strictly needed. All variables in equations refer to contemporaneous objects.

5. The relevance of financial institutions as liquidity-creation engines was well known to Irving Fisher (1912). See citation at the outset.

6. Stockman (1981) examines a liquidity-in-advance constraint on firms' investment, which is close to the present formulation. However, he confines his attention to the case in which cash is the only medium of exchange. Stockman's model will be extended to account for endogenous growth and liquid bonds later in the chapter.

7. To simplify the exposition, r will initially be treated as exogenous and constant over time. The appendix at the end of this chapter provides a general equilibrium example where at steady state r is equal to the (exogenous) rate of time preference.

8. The standard yardsticks for measuring price deflation are the CPI or PPI, which largely ignore the real estate sector.

9. This result is in line with Gertler and Karadi (2011) in the context of a very different model.

10. Notice that the negative results of QE in exchange for toxic assets stressed in the text could be exacerbated if removing toxic assets from the private sector lowers their popularity as collateral in credit contracts, for example. This would correspond to a network effect of the type discussed in Uribe (1997) in regard to currency substitution. Endogenizing θ is a major task that deserves special treatment and will not be pursued here. For a partial attempt in that direction, inspired by the subprime crisis, see Calvo (2012b).

11. Caballero and Farhi (2015) reach similar conclusions in the context of an entirely different model focused on safe assets.

12. The model discussed here is a close relative to Stockman (1981), but the latter utilizes a Solow model in which long-term growth is independent of the opportunity cost of liquidity (i.e., *inflation* in Stockman 1981).

13. Land market price is hit by changes in τ. Hence its collateral value is sensitive to a liquidity crunch. This weakness in the model can easily be fixed by assuming that the missing factor is putty-putty capital.

14. Local uniqueness requires more stringent conditions. In Calvo (1979) where money is assumed to be an argument in the production function in a closed economy context, it is shown that local uniqueness requires that the elasticity of output with respect to real monetary balances *times* the coefficient of relative risk aversion in consumption is less than one.

Introduction to Part II

1. The sample in the chapter ends with 2004. It would be interesting to check if these results would hold in the Lehman crisis.

2. In Calvo, Izquierdo, and Loo-Kung (2013) we replace DLD with DLD net of (gross) international reserves, with equivalent results.

3. Satellite economies in the eurozone also suffered SS (see Merler and Pisani-Ferry 2012), but the impact was much less because these economies had the support of the ECB, a consequence of financial integration. This example shows, by the way, that "financial integration" is a complex concept, which is unlikely to be given full justice by a single indicator.

Chapter 6

1. Calvo et al. (2006) call these credit-less recovery episodes "Phoenix Miracles."

2. The list of countries includes Algeria, Argentina, Brazil, Bulgaria, Chile, Colombia, Dominican Republic, Ecuador, El Salvador, Indonesia, Ivory Coast, Lebanon, Malaysia, Mexico, Morocco, Nigeria, Panama, Peru, Philippines, Russia, South Africa, South Korea, Thailand, Tunisia, Turkey, Uruguay, and Venezuela.

3. The capital flow window is constructed following the methodology detailed in Calvo, Izquierdo, and Mejia (2008). Data to construct the monthly proxy of capital flows were collected from the International Monetary Fund dataset. For the systemic spread window, given that the EMBI is not available for the 1980s, we use the federal funds rate instead as a proxy that captures the cost of international financing for EMs. This is a reasonable assumption since bank credit was the dominant source of funding for EMs during that period. See Calvo, Izquierdo, and Talvi (2006) and Ortiz et al. (2009) for the dates of these systemic windows.

4. Data on banking crises and debt default/rescheduling are from Reinhart and Rogoff (2009).

5. Mendoza (2010) documents the dynamics of Tobin's q following Sudden Stop episodes. Nakamura et al. (2013) study the asset pricing implications of consumption disasters, including some of the episodes mentioned in this chapter.

6. Following Calvo, Coricelli, and Ottonello (2012) we define a high inflation (low inflation) denotes the set of episodes in which the maximum level of annual CPI inflation during the episode was above (below) 30 percent.

7. For a recent study in this direction showing the importance of wage rigidity in a crisis environment, see Schmitt-Grohe and Uribe (2014).

8. An increase the real exchange rate is equivalent to a real depreciation of the domestic currency.

9. For instance, Kehoe and Prescott (2007) documents several significant post-crisis policy revisions.

10. See chapter 5 for a model consistent with these results.

11. In particular, we assume a Cobb–Douglas production function and compute the log changes in measured TFP $(\hat{a}_t)$:

$$\log\left(\frac{\hat{a}_t}{\hat{a}_{t-1}}\right) = \log\left(\frac{y_t}{y_{t-1}}\right) - \alpha\log\left(\frac{k_t}{k_{t-1}}\right) - (1-\alpha)\left(\frac{l_t}{l_{t-1}}\right),$$

where y_t denotes output in period t, k_t denotes capital, and l_t denotes employment. Given the lack of data on hours worked or utilization of capital for this sample of EMs, measured TFP will also capture variation of input services.

12. Interestingly, the recovery of TFP seems to be lower than the recovery of output: once output recovers its pre-crisis level TFP is 4 percent below its pre-crisis level (significant at the 5 percent level) and factor inputs 3 percent above their pre-crisis level.

Chapter 7

1. This chapter is a slightly modified version of NBER Working Paper 14026, May 2008. We wish to thank Esteban Verdugo for his valuable assistance.

2. Variable ω is a measure of the economy's ability to finance domestic absorption of tradable goods. Although it could be claimed that ω is a

measure of trade openness, it should be noted that it is significantly different from the standard one, that is, the ratio of exports plus imports to GDP (see the last section for more details).

3. This equation could be derived from first principles if H and Z are identified with consumption of nontradables and tradables, the intertemporal utility function is separable, and the utility function is iso-elastic in H and Z.

4. It should be pointed out, however, that a large increase in rer is likely to generate financial difficulties even when there are no foreign-exchange denominated debts, as in the case of firms that depend on imported raw materials.

5. In a world of heterogeneous agents, full-fledged Sudden Stops could take place even under current account *surplus* because there could be key sectors that exhibit a current account deficit while the rest of the economy exhibits an even larger surplus. In our sample about 5 percent of Sudden Stops occur under a current account surplus the period prior to crisis. This is another reason why equation (6) is likely to underestimate the required change in rer of an incipient Sudden Stop.

6. A margin call could be due to the fall in the price of asset holdings from a particular country.

7. This can occur when the variance of returns to investment projects in EMs is high relative to the variance of the liquidity shock to informed investors (see Calvo 1999).

8. Sudden Stops could also be rationalized in terms of models displaying a unique equilibrium, as long as the equilibrium outcome is a discontinuous function of fundamentals. For example, Calvo (2003) shows that there could exist a critical level of government debt beyond which the economy plunges into an equilibrium that displays Sudden Stop features. Calvo (2003) is a non-monetary model, where public debt is denominated in terms of tradables. Thus liability dollarization is actually assumed for the entire debt, implying that the higher the degree of liability dollarization (measured in this model by the public debt/output ratio), the higher the probability that a given negative shock will generate a Sudden Stop.

9. Uniqueness could also be obtained along the lines suggested by Morris and Shin (1998). Consider the limit case in which informational noise (ε in their notation) goes to zero, and let currency devaluation after crisis be an increasing function of the degree of liability dollarization. Then the likelihood of a crisis due to a deterioration in *fundamentals* (θ in their notation) would be higher, the higher the degree of liability dollarization.

10. For an explicit derivation of the relationship between CAD/Z and $1 - \omega$, see last section of this chapter.

11. Using a panel of 105 countries for the period 1970 to 1991, they conclude that the current account has no significance in explaining currency crises.

12. Kaminsky and Reinhart (1999) implicitly introduce a link between current account performance and currency crises by incorporating the growth rate of imports and exports in their analysis. They select the latter as a relevant early warning indicator of currency crises based on noise-to-signal ratio properties of the series.

13. This analysis does find that under some definitions of currency crisis, and particularly excluding African countries, current account deficits are a significant determinant of the probability of experiencing currency crises.

14. They focus on large RER swings to define a crisis.

15. According to our definition, for example, Argentina's Sudden Stop starts in May 1999 whereas the currency crisis only hits in February 2002.

16. Exceeding 5 percent of GDP.

17. Moreover this study expands the sample of countries from 32 to 110 given availability of new data on dollarization. The larger and more heterogeneous sample made us introduce controls for financial integration in the estimations, which turned out to be significant, as we report in last section of this chapter.

18. Besides, as it will become evident later on, from an integrated capital market perspective, it is not crucial whether domestic or foreign investors are responsible for the cut in financing in terms of the consequences that the withdrawal of funds will pose on the real exchange rate and the associated balance-sheet effects.

19. Both the first and second moments of the series are calculated each period using an expanding window with a minimum of 24 (months of) observations and a start date fixed at January 1990. This intends to capture a learning process or updating of the behavior of the series.

20. As a result a Sudden Stop phase starts with a fall in capital flows exceeding one standard deviation, followed by a fall of two standard deviations. The process lasts until the change in capital flows is bigger than minus one standard deviation.

21. See the data appendix for definitions and sources of these variables. All series are measured in constant 2000 US dollars.

22. More specifically, we use JPMorgan's Emerging Market Bond Index (EMBI) spread over US Treasury bonds for developing countries, the Merrill Lynch euro-area Government Index spreads for euro-area countries (as well as Nordic countries such as Denmark, Norway, and Sweden), and G7 Government Index spreads for all remaining developed countries.

23. The first two years of observations are lost, given that such information is used to construct initial standard deviations.

24. The distinction between EMBI+ and other developing countries is made because their levels of financial integration differ and thus bunching behavior may differ.

25. For a detailed treatment of the Latin American episodes, see Calvo, Izquierdo, and Talvi (2002).

26. An increase means a real depreciation of the currency.

27. Our sample of countries is also different and much larger than that in Arteta (2003).

28. In a related study, Cavallo and Frankel (2004), using a similar definition of Sudden Stop to that in Calvo, Izquierdo, and Mejia (2004), also introduce measures of dollarization more akin to those in Arteta (2003). These alternative measures provide mixed results in terms of their contribution to the likelihood of a Sudden Stop. It is also worth mentioning that our approach focuses on the impact of dollarization on the likelihood of a Sudden Stop, rather than on the consequences of dollarization and Sudden Stops on relevant variables such as economic growth, as in Edwards (2003).

29. Evidence on currency matching of bank assets and liabilities for EMs can be found in Inter-American Development Bank (2004).

30. Based on information used in Inter-American Development Bank (2004).

31. The use of a Probit model and the construction of a dichotomous Sudden Stop variable are due to our belief that large and unexpected capital flow reversals have nonlinear effects, as they trigger substantial balance-sheet fluctuations that may lead to serious credit constraints or plain bankruptcies. An alternative, which is not explored in this chapter, would be to use regime-switching models.

32. Particular attention will be paid to estimation problems that arise from the inclusion of potentially endogenous variables within a Probit with random effects. See both the robustness section as well as the technical appendix for a discussion.

33. Except for terms-of-trade growth, a variable that enters contemporaneously in our estimations.

34. For illustration purposes, we use estimations shown in column 7 of table A2 of the appendix to construct this figure.

35. Other developing countries are roughly evenly split above and below the median.

36. Debt stocks are not included because they are partly captured by public external debt and bank foreign borrowing (via their participation in DLD).

37. Given the way the index was originally constructed, a higher value indicates less exchange rate flexibility.

38. See Calvo, Izquierdo, and Talvi (2002) for a more detailed discussion.

39. An example backing this assertion is the case of Korea, where public sector debt represented only 10 percent of GDP prior to its 1997 Sudden Stop, before quadrupling once the financial sector bailout was added to the fiscal burden.

40. In part, this result may be due to the lack of control groups (i.e., other developing and developed countries for which IIF does not report data). Results are available on request.

41. Probit models can be reduced to latent variable models. For the case where endogeneity in $1 - \omega$ is suspected, a system of two equations can be defined, one representing the latent variable behind the Sudden Stop variable (which is assumed to be a linear function of all variables in the Probit, including $1 - \omega$), the other representing $1 - \omega$, which is considered to be a linear function of all other variables included in the Probit estimation, as well as a lag in $1 - \omega$. Residuals from this second regression are included in the Probit regression to determine their significance. If the latter are significant, endogeneity cannot be rejected. For further details, see Rivers and Vuong (1988), or Wooldridge (2002).

42. Following the Rivers–Vuong approach, in the first stage we used all the other explanatory variables in the Probit equation and the second lag of ω as instruments of the potentially endogenous variable (ω_{t-1}).

43. None of the previous point estimates of the coefficient accompanying $1 - \omega$ in appendix table A2 fall within the confidence interval shown in appendix table A3.

44. Ranciere et al. (2006) show that while developing countries may be exposed to crises, there are still long-term benefits stemming from financial

liberalization. Their empirical findings show that financial liberalization fosters economic growth at the cost of a higher propensity to crises. Overall, they find a positive net effect of financial liberalization on growth.

45. These estimations already control for endogeneity in $1 - \omega$ and use bootstrapped confidence intervals.

46. Relevant work in this direction has recently been conducted by Edwards (2003), Ranciere, Tornell and Westermann (2006), but balance-sheet effects still need to be incorporated into this line of research. Work by Calvo, Izquierdo, and Loo-Kung (2013) suggests that DLD net of foreign reserves as a share of GDP also works as a significant determinant of the probability of a Systemic Sudden Stop. This result is used to compute an optimal level of international reserves that balances the costs of holding reserves against the benefit of lowering the probability of Sudden Stop.

References

Aghion, Philippe, Philippe Bacchetta, and Abhijit Banerjee. 2001. Currency crises and monetary policy in an economy with credit constraints. *European Economic Review* 45:1121–1150.

Agosin, Manuel R., and Franklin Huaita. 2012. Overreaction in capital flows to emerging markets: Booms and sudden stops. *Journal of International Money and Finance* 31:1140–1155.

Aguiar, Mark, and Gita Gopinath. 2007. Emerging market business cycles: The cycle is the trend. *Journal of Political Economy* 115 (1): 69–102.

Arellano, Cristina, and Enrique Mendoza. 2002. Credit frictions and sudden stops in small open economies: An equilibrium business cycle framework for emerging market crises. NBER working paper 8880.

Arteta, Carlos O. 2003. Are financially dollarized countries more prone to costly crises? International finance discussion paper 763. Board of Governors of the Federal Reserve System.

Bagehot, Walter. 1873. *Lombard Street: A Description of the Money Market.* New York: Wiley.

Barclays. 2015. *China, Beyond SDR: RMB as a Safe Asset.* Emerging Markets Research, May 15. London.

Berger, David. 2012. Countercyclical restructuring and jobless recoveries. Unpublished manuscript. Yale University.

Bernanke, B. S. 2009. On the outlook for the economy and policy. http://www.federalreserve.gov/newsevents/speech/bernanke20091116a.htm.

Bernanke, Ben S., and Mark Gertler. 1989. Agency costs, net worth, and business fluctuations. *American Economic Review* 79 (1): 14–31.

Bernanke, Ben S., Mark Gertler, and Simon Gilchrist. 1999. The financial accelerator in a quantitative business cycle framework. vol. 15. Ed. J. B. Taylor and M. Woodford, 1341–1393. Handbook of Macroeconomics. Amsterdam: Elsevier, North-Holland.

Bernanke, Ben S., and Mark Gertler. 1989. Agency costs, net worth, and business fluctuations. *American Economic Review* 79 (1): 14–31.

Bianchi, Javier. 2011. Overborrowing and systemic externalities in the business cycle. *American Economic Review* 101 (7): 3400–3426.

Bloom, Nick, Stephen Bond, and John Van Reenen. 2007. Uncertainty and investment dynamics. *Review of Economic Studies* 74 (2): 391–415.

Bordo, Michael. 2007. Growing up to financial stability. NBER working paper 12993.

Brunnermeier, Markus K. 2009. Deciphering the liquidity and credit crunch 2007–2008. *Journal of Economic Perspectives* 23 (1): 77–100.

Brunnermeier, Markus K., and Isabel Schnabel. 2015. Bubbles, capital flows, credit, macroprudential policy, monetary policy. CEPR working paper. April.

Brunnermeier, Markus K., and Yuliy Sannikov. 2014. Forthcoming. A macroeconomic model with a financial sector. *American Economic Review* 104 (2): 379–421.

Bruno, Valentina, and Hyun Song Shin. 2014. Assessing macroprudential policies: The case of South Korea. *Scandinavian Journal of Economics* 116 (1): 128–157.

Buera, Francisco J., and Benjamin Moll. 2015. Aggregate implications of a credit crunch: The importance of heterogeneity. *American Economic Journal. Macroeconomics* 7 (3): 1–42.

Buffie, Edward F., and Manoj Atolia. 2012. Resurrecting the weak credibility hypothesis in models of exchange-rate-based stabilization. *European Economic Review* 56 (3): 361–372.

Burstein, Ariel, and Gita Gopinath. 2014. International prices and exchange rates. In *Handbook of International Economics*. vol. 4. Ed. G. Gopinha, E. Helpman and K. Rogoff, 391–451. Amsterdam: Elsevier, North-Holland.

Caballero, Ricardo J., and Emmanuel Farhi. 2015. The safety trap. Unpublished manuscript. MIT.

Caballero, Ricardo J., Emmanuel Farhi, and Pierre-Olivier Gourinchas. 2008. An equilibrium model of global imbalances and low interest rates. *American Economic Review* 98 (1): 358–393.

Caballero, Ricardo, and Stavros Panageas. 2003. *Hedging sudden stops and precautionary recessions: A quantitative framework*. Mimeo. MIT.

Calomiris, Charles W. 2009. Financial innovation, regulation and reform. *Cato Journal* 29 (1): 65–91.

Calvo, Guillermo. 1978. On the time consistency of optimal policy in a monetary economy. *Econometrica* 46 (November): 1411–1428.

Calvo, Guillermo. 1979. On models of money and perfect foresight. *International Economic Review* 20 (1): 83–103.

Calvo, Guillermo. 1983. Staggered prices in a utility maximizing framework. *Journal of Monetary Economics* 12 (September): 383–398.

Calvo, Guillermo. 1996. *Money, Exchange Rates, and Output*. Cambridge: MIT Press.

Calvo, Guillermo A. 1998. Capital flows and capital-market crises: The simple economics of sudden stops. [Reprinted in Guillermo A. Calvo, *Emerging Capital Markets in Turmoil: Bad Luck or Bad Policy*, Cambridge: MIT Press, 2005.] *Journal of Applied Economics* 1 (1): 35–54.

Calvo, Guillermo A. 1999. Contagion in emerging markets: When Wall Street is a carrier. Mimeo. University of Maryland. (Partial version in *Proceedings from the Congress of the International Economic Association*, Buenos Aires, Argentina, 2002. Full version in Guillermo A. Calvo, *Emerging Capital Markets in Turmoil: Bad Luck or Bad Policy*, Cambridge: MIT Press, 2005.)

Calvo, Guillermo A. 2003. Explaining Sudden Stop, growth collapse, and BOP crisis: The case of distortionary output taxes. *IMF Staff Papers* 50. Special Issue. (Reprint in Guillermo A. Calvo, *Emerging Capital Markets in Turmoil: Bad Luck or Bad Policy*, Cambridge: MIT Press, 2005.)

Calvo, Guillermo. 2005. *Emerging Capital Markets in Turmoil: Bad Luck or Bad Policy?* Cambridge: MIT Press.

Calvo, Guillermo. 2012a. The Price Theory of Money, Prospero's liquidity trap, and Sudden Stop: Back to basics and back. NBER discussion paper 18285.

Calvo, Guillermo. 2012b. Financial crises and liquidity shocks: A bank-run perspective. *European Economic Review* 56 (April): 317–326.

Calvo, Guillermo. 2013. Puzzling over the anatomy of crises: Liquidity and the veil of finance. Monetary and Economic Studies, Bank of Japan, (November): 39–63 (working paper available at www.columbia.edu/~gc2286).

Calvo, Guillermo. 2014. Sudden Stop and Sudden Flood of foreign direct investment: Inverse bank run, output and welfare distribution. *Scandinavian Journal of Economics* 110 (1): 5–19.

Calvo, Guillermo A., Fabrizio Coricelli, and Pablo Ottonello. 2012. Labor market, financial crises and inflation: Jobless and wageless recoveries. Working paper 18480.

Calvo, Guillermo, Fabrizio Coricelli, and Pablo Ottonello. 2013. Jobless recoveries during financial crises: Is inflation the way out? NBER working paper 19683. (Forthcoming in Sofia Bauducco, Lawrence Christiano and Claudio Raddatz, eds., Macroeconomic and Financial Stability: Challenges for Monetary Policy. Santiago: Central Bank of Chile.)

Calvo, Guillermo A., Alejandro Izquierdo, and Ernesto Talvi. 2002. Sudden Stops, the real exchange rate and fiscal sustainability: Argentina's lessons. NBER working paper 9828. (Reprint in Guillermo A. Calvo, *Emerging Capital Markets in Turmoil: Bad Luck or Bad Policy*, Cambridge: MIT Press, 2005.)

Calvo, Guillermo A., Alejandro Izquierdo, and Ernesto Talvi. 2006. Phoenix miracles in emerging markets: recovering without credit from systemic financial crises. NBER working paper 12101.

Calvo, Guillermo A., Alejandro Izquierdo, and Luis Fernando Mejia. 2004. On the empirics of Sudden Stops: The relevance of balance-sheet effects. NBER working paper 10520.

Calvo, Guillermo, Alejandro Izquierdo, and Luis-Fernando Mejia. 2008. Systemic Sudden Stop: The relevance of balance-sheet effects and financial integration. NBER working paper 14026.

Calvo, Guillermo A., Alejandro Izquierdo, and Rudy Loo-Kung. 2006. Relative price volatility under Sudden Stops: The relevance of balance sheet effects. *Journal of International Economics* 69 (1): 231–254.

Calvo, Guillermo, Alejandro Izquierdo, and Rudy Loo-Kung. 2013 Optimal holdings of international reserves: Self-insurance against Sudden Stop.

Monetaria, Centro de Estudios Monetarios Latinoamericanos (January–June): 1–35.

Calvo, Guillermo, and Rudy Loo-Kung. 2011. US recovery: A new "phoenix miracle"? VOX-EU http://www.voxeu.org/article/us-recovery-new-phoenix-miracle.

Calvo, Guillermo, Leiderman Leonardo, and Carmen M. Reinhart. 2005. 1993. Capital inflows and real exchange rate appreciation in Latin America: The role of external factors. Staff Papers. March. (Reprint in Calvo 2005.)

Calvo, Guillermo, and Carmen M. Reinhart. 2000. Fixing for your life. [Washington, DC: Bookings Institution.] *Brookings Trade Forum*, 1–57.

Calvo, Guillermo, and Carmen M. Reinhart. 2002. Fear of floating. *Quarterly Journal of Economics* 117 (2): 379–408.

Calvo, Guillermo, and Carlos A. Végh. 1995. Fighting inflation with high interest rates: The small-open-economy under flexible prices. *Journal of Money, Credit and Banking* 27:49–66.

Calvo, Guillermo, and Carlos A. Végh. 1999. Inflation stabilization and BOP crises in developing countries. In J. B. Taylor and M. Woodford, eds., Handbook of Macroeconomics, vol. 1C. Amsterdam: Elsevier, North-Holland, 1531–1614.

Canzoneri, Matthew, and Bezhad Diba. 2005. Interest rate rules and price determinacy: The role of transactions services of bonds. *Journal of Monetary Economics* 52 (2): 329–344.

Canzoneri, Matthew, Robert E. Cumby, Bezhad Diba, and David Lopez-Salido. 2008. Monetary aggregates and liquidity in a neo-Wicksellian framework. *Journal of Money, Credit and Banking* 40 (8): 1667–1698.

Carlson, Benny, and Lars Jonung. 2002. Ohlin on the Great Depression: The popular message in the daily press. In *Bertil Ohlin: A Centennial Celebration (1899–1999)*, ed. R. Findlay, L. Jonung and M. Lundah, 263–301. Cambridge: MIT Press.

Cavallo, Eduardo, and Jeffrey Frankel. J. 2004. Does openness to trade make countries more vulnerable to Sudden Stops, or less? Using gravity to establish causality. NBER working paper 10957.

Cerra, Valerie, and Sweta Chaman Saxena. 2008. Growth dynamics: The myth of economic recovery. *American Economic Review* 98 (1): 439–457.

Choudhri, E. U., and S. Dalia. Hakura, 2001. Exchange rate pass-through to domestic prices: Does the inflationary environment matter? IMF working paper WP/01/194.

Christiano, Lawrence J., and Terry J. Fitzgerald. 2000. Understanding the fiscal Theory of the Price Level. *Federal Reserve Bank of Cleveland. Economic Review (Federal Reserve Bank of Atlanta)* 36 (2).

Christiano, Lawrence J., Roberto Motto, and Massimo Rostagno. 2014. Risk shocks. *American Economic Review* 104 (1): 27–65.

Christiano, Lawrence, and Daisuke Ikeda. 2013. Leverage restrictions in a business cycle model. NBER working paper 18688.

Cochrane, John H. 2011. Determinacy and identification with Taylor rules. *Journal of Political Economy* 119 (3): 565–615.

Cole, H., and L. Ohanian. 1999. The Great Depression in the United States from a neoclassical perspective. *Federal Reserve Bank of Minneapolis Quarterly Review* (Winter): 2–24.

Corsetti, Giancarlo, Paolo Pesenti, and Nouriel Roubini. 2001. Fundamental determinants of the Asian crisis: The role of financial fragility and external imbalances. In *Regional and Global Capital Flows: Macroeconomic Causes and Consequences*, ed. A. Krueger and T. Ito, 11–41. Chicago: University of Chicago Press.

Cowan, K., and J. De Gregorio. 2005. International borrowing, capital controls and the exchange rate lessons from Chile. NBER working paper 11382.

Dabús, Carlos. 2000. Inflationary regimes and relative price variability: Evidence from Argentina. *Journal of Development Economics* 62 (2): 535–547.

Davidson, Paul. 1965. Keynes's finance motive. *Oxford Economic Papers. New Series* 17 (1): 47–65.

Davison, A., and D. Hinkley. 1997. *Bootstrap Methods and Their Applications.* Cambridge, UK: Cambridge University Press.

Diamond, Douglas W., and Philip H. Dybvig. 1983. Bank runs, deposit insurance and liquidity. *Journal of Political Economy* 91 (3): 401–419.

Dornbusch, R., and S. Fischer. 1993. Moderate inflation. *World Bank Economic Review* 7 (1): 1–44.

Dornbusch, Rudiger. 1987. Exchange rate and prices. *American Economic Review* 77 (1): 93–106.

Edwards, Sebastian. 2001. Does the current account matter? NBER working paper 8275.

Edwards, Sebastian. 2003. Current account imbalances: History, trends and adjustment mechanisms. Fourth Mundell–Fleming Lecture at IMF. November 6, 2003.

Edwards, Sebastian. 2004. Thirty years of current account imbalances, current account reversals and sudden stops. NBER working paper 10276.

Eichengreen, Barry, and Andrew Rose. 1998. Staying afloat when the wind shifts: External factors and emerging-market banking crises. NBER working paper 6370.

Eichengreen, Barry, Ricardo Hausmann, and Ugo Panizza. 2005. The pain of original sin. In *Other People's Money: Debt Denomination and Financial Instability in Emerging Market Economies*, ed. B. Eichengreen and R. Hausmann. Chicago: University of Chicago Press.

Feenstra, Robert C., Robert Inklaar, and Marcel P. Timmer. 2013. The next generation of the Penn World Table. Available for download at www.ggdc.net/pwt.

Financial Times. 2014. Bonds: Anatomy of a market meltdown. November 17.

Fischer, Stanley. 1974. Money and production. *Economic Inquiry* 12 (4): 517–533.

Fisher, Irving. 2006. *The Purchasing Power of Money: Its Determination and Relation to Credit, Interest, and Crises*. New York: Cosimo. (1912).

Fisher, Irving. 1933. The debt-deflation theory of Great Depressions. *Econometrica* 1 (4): 337–357.

Fisher, Irving. 2012. *The Money Illusion*. New York: Start Publishing LLC.

Foucault, Thierry, Marco Pagano, and Ailsa Röel. 2013. *Market Liquidity: Theory, Evidence and Policy*. Oxford, UK: Oxford University Press.

Frankel, Jeffrey, and Andrew Rose. 1996. Currency crashes in emerging markets: An empirical treatment. *Journal of International Economics* 41 (3/4): 351–366.

Friedman, Milton. 1977. Nobel Lecture: Inflation and unemployment. *Journal of Political Economy* 85 (3): 451–472.

Friedman, Milton. 1994. *Money Mischief: Episodes in Monetary History.* Orlando, FL: Harcourt Brace.

Friedman, Milton, and Anna J. Schwartz. 1963. *A Monetary History of the United States, 1867–1960.* Princeton: Princeton University Press.

Fuentes, Miguel A., Claudio E. Raddatz, and Carmen M. Reinhart. 2014. An overview. In *Capital Mobility and Monetary Policy*, ed. M. A. Fuentes, C. E. Raddatz and C. M. Reinhart. Santiago: Central Bank of Chile.

Furceri, D., and A. Mourougane. 2009. The effects of financial crises on potential output: New empirical evidence from OECD countries. OECD Economics Department working paper 669.

Gantmacher, F. R. 1956. *The Theory of Matrices.* New York: Chelsea Publishing.

Geanakoplos, John. 2010. The leverage cycle. In *NBER Macroeconomics Annual 2009*, ed. D. Acemoglu, K. Rogoff and M. Woodford, 1–65. Chicago: University of Chicago Press.

Gertler, Mark, and Nobuhiro Kiyotaki. 2010. Financial intermediation and credit policy in business cycle analysis. In *Handbook of Monetary Economics, vol. 3A*, ed. B. Friedman and M. Woodford, 547–599. Amsterdam: Elsevier.

Gertler, Mark, and Peter Karadi. 2011. A model of unconventional monetary policy. *Journal of Monetary Economics* 58:17–34.

Gopinath, Gita, and Brent Neiman. 2013. Trade adjustment and productivity in large crises. *American Economic Review* 104 (3): 793–831.

Gopinath, Gita, Oleg Itskhoki, and Roberto Rigobon. 2010. Currency choice and exchange rate pass-through. *American Economic Review* 100 (1): 304–336.

Gorton, Gary, and Andrew Metrick. 2012. Securitized banking and the run on repo. *Journal of Financial Economics* 104:425–451.

Guilkey, D., and J. Murphy. 1993. Estimation and testing in the random effects Probit model. *Journal of Econometrics* 59:301–317.

Hahn, F. H. 1965. On some problems of proving the existence of an equilibrium in a monetary economy. In *The Theory of Interest Rates*, ed. F. H. Hahn and F. P. R. Brechling, 126–135. London: Macmillan.

Hayek, Friedrich August von, 1974. The pretence of knowledge. Nobel Prize Lecture.

Heckman, J. 1981. Statistical models for discrete panel data. In *Structural Analysis of Discrete Data with Econometric Applications*, ed. C. Manksi and D. McFadden, 114–178. Cambridge: MIT Press.

Hicks, John R. 1937. Mr. Keynes and the classics: A suggested interpretation. *Econometrica* 5 (2): 147–159.

Hicks, John R. 1982. *Money, Interest and Wages*. Cambridge: Harvard University Press.

Holmström, Bengt. 2015. Understanding the role of debt in the financial system. BIS working paper 479.

Holmström, Bengt, and Jean Tirole. 1998. Private and public supply of liquidity. *Journal of Political Economy* 106 (11): 1–39.

Holmström, Bengt, and Jean Tirole. 2011. *Inside and Outside Liquidity*. Cambridge: MIT Press.

Honohan, Patrick, and Anqing Shi. 2002. Deposit dollarization and the financial sector in emerging economies. World Bank working paper 2748.

Hsiao, C. 2003. *Analysis of Panel Data*. 2nd ed. Cambridge, UK: Cambridge University Press.

IMF. 1999. Monetary policy in a dollarized economies, Occasional paper 171.

Inter-American Development Bank. 2004. *Unlocking Credit: The Quest for Deep and Stable Bank Lending. Economic and Social Progress in Latin America Report*. Baltimore: Johns Hopkins University Press.

Izquierdo, Alejandro. 1999. Credit constraints, and the asymmetric behavior of output and asset prices under external shocks. PhD dissertation. University of Maryland.

Izquierdo, Alejandro. 2013. Sudden Stops in Capital Flows. In *The Evidence and Impact of Financial Globalization*, ed. G. Caprio. Amsterdam: Elsevier.

Jaimovich, Nir, and Henry E. Siu. 2012. The trend is the cycle: Job polarization and jobless recoveries. NBER working paper 18334.

Jordà, Òscar, Moritz Schularick, and Alan M. Taylor. 2015. Leveraged bubbles. NBER conference paper. June.

Kaminsky, Graciela L., and Carmen M. Reinhart. 1999. The twin crises: The causes of banking and balance-of-payments problems. *American Economic Review* 89 (3): 473–500.

Kehoe, Timothy Jerome, and Edward C. Prescott. 2007. *Great Depressions of the twentieth century. Research Department.* Federal Reserve Bank of Minneapolis.

Keynes, John M. 1961. *The General Theory of Employment, Interest and Money.* London: Macmillan. (1936).

Khan, Aubhik, and Julia K. Thomas. 2013. Credit shocks and aggregate fluctuations in an economy with production heterogeneity. *Journal of Political Economy* 121 (6): 1055–1107.

Kiyotaki, Nobuhiro, and John Moore. 1997. Credit cycles. *Journal of Political Economy* 105 (2): 211–248.

Knight, Frank H. 1921. *Risk, Uncertainty, and Profit.* Chicago: University of Chicago Press.

Korinek, Anton, and Enrique G. Mendoza. 2013. From sudden stops to Fisherian deflation: Quantitative theory and policy implications. NBER working paper 19362.

Krishnamurthy, Arvind, and Annette Vissing-Jorgensen. 2013. The ins and outs of LSAPs. Presented at the Jackson Hole conference. August 9, 2013.

Krugman, Paul R. 1979. A model of balance-of-payments crises. *Journal of Money, Credit and Banking* 11 (August): 311–325.

Kuhn, Thomas S. 1962. *The Structure of Scientific Revolutions.* Chicago: Chicago University Press.

Kydland, Finn, and Edward C. Prescott. 1977. Rules rather than discretion: The inconsistency of optimal plans. *Journal of Political Economy* 85:473–493.

Lane, Phillip R., and Gian Maria Milesi-Ferreti. 2006. The external wealth of nations mark II: Revised and extended estimates of foreign assets and liabilities, 1970–2004. IIIS discussion paper 126.

Leeper, Eric M. 1991. Equilibrium under "active" and "passive" monetary and fiscal policies. *Journal of Monetary Economics* 27:129–147.

Levhari, D., and D. Patinkin. 1968. The role of money in a simple growth model. *American Economic Review* 58 (September): 713–753.

Levy-Yeyati, Eduardo, and Federico Sturzenegger. 2005. Classifying exchange rate regimes: Deeds vs. words. *European Economic Review* 49 (6): 1603–1635.

Levy-Yeyati, Eduardo. 2006. Financial dollarisation: Evaluating the consequences. *Economic Policy* 21 (45): 61–118.

Mehrling, Perry. 2010. *The New Lombard Street: How the Fed Became the Dealer of Last Resort*. Princeton: Princeton University Press.

Mendoza, Enrique G. 2006. Endogenous sudden stops in a business cycle model with collateral constraints: A Fisherian deflation of Tobin's q. NBER working paper 12564.

Mendoza, Enrique G. 2010. Sudden stops, financial crises, and leverage. *American Economic Review* 100 (5): 1941–1966.

Mendoza, Enrique G., and Marco E. Terrones. 2012. An anatomy of credit booms and their demise. NBER working paper 18379.

Mendoza, Enrique G. 2010. Sudden stops, financial crises, and leverage. *American Economic Review* 100 (5): 1941–1966.

Mendoza, Enrique G., Vincenzo Quadrini, and José-Víctor Ríos-Rull. 2009. Financial integration, financial development, and global imbalances. *Journal of Political Economy* 117 (3): 371–416.

Merler, S., and Jean Pisani-Ferry. 2012. Sudden stops in the euro area. *Bruegel Policy Contribution* (2012/06, March).

Meza, Felipe, and Erwan Quintin. 2007. Factor utilization and the real impact of financial crises. *B.E. Journal of Macroeconomics* 7 (1): 1–39.

Midrigan, Virgiliu, and Daniel Yi Xu. 2014. Finance and misallocation: Evidence from plant-level data. *American Economic Review* 104 (2): 422–458.

Milesi-Ferretti, Gian Maria, and Assaf Razin. 2000. Current account reversals and currency crises: Empirical regularities. In *Currency Crises*, ed. P. Krugman, 285–323. Chicago: University of Chicago Press.

Minsky, Hyman P. 2008a. *Stabilizing an Unstable Economy*. New York: McGraw Hill.

Minsky, Hyman P. 2008b. *John Maynard Keynes*. New York: McGraw Hill.

Mishkin, Frederic S. 2006. *The Next Great Globalization: How Disadvantaged Nations Can Harness Their Financial Systems to Get Rich.* Princeton: Princeton University Press.

Morris, Stephen, and Hyun Song Shin. 1998. Unique equilibrium in a model of self-fulfilling currency attacks. *American Economic Review* 88 (3): 587–597.

Nakamura, Emi, Jón Steinsson, Robert Barro, and José Ursúa. 2013. Crises and recoveries in an empirical model of consumption disasters. *American Economic Journal. Macroeconomics* 5 (3): 35–74.

Neumeyer, Pablo A., and Fabrizio Perri. 2005. Business cycles in emerging economies: The role of interest rates. *Journal of Monetary Economics* 52 (2): 345–380.

Oberfield, Ezra. 2013. Productivity and misallocation during a crisis: Evidence from the Chilean crisis of 1982. *Review of Economic Dynamics* 16 (1): 100–119.

Obstfeld, Maurice. 1986. Rational and self-fulfilling balance-of-payments crisis. *American Economic Review* 76 (March): 72–81.

Obstfeld, Maurice, and Kenneth Rogoff. 1983. Speculative hyperinflations in maximizing models: Can we rule them out? *Journal of Political Economy* 91 (4): 675–687.

Obstfeld, Maurice, and Kenneth Rogoff. 1986. Ruling out divergent speculative bubbles. *Journal of Monetary Economics* 17 (May): 346–362.

Obstfeld, Maurice, Jay C. Shambaugh, and Alan M. Taylor. 2010. Financial stability, the trilemma, and international reserves. *American Economic Journal. Macroeconomics* 2 (2): 57–94.

Ottonello, Pablo. 2014. *Capital unemployment, financial shocks, and investment slumps.* Mimeo. Columbia University.

Patinkin, Don. 1949. The indeterminacy of absolute prices in classical economic theory. *Econometrica* 17 (1): 1–27.

Patinkin, Don. 1965. *Money, Interest, and Prices.* New York: Harper and Row.

Pratap, Sangeeta, and Carlos Urrutia. 2012. Financial frictions and total factor productivity: Accounting for the real effects of financial crises. *Review of Economic Dynamics* 15 (3): 336–358.

Queraltó, Albert. 2013. A model of slow recoveries from financial crises. FRB International Finance Discussion Paper 1097.

Radelet, Steven, and Jeffrey Sachs. 1998. The East Asian financial crisis: Diagnosis, remedies, prospects. *Brookings Paper* 28 (1): 1–74.

Ranciere, Romain, Aaron Tornell, and Frank Westermann. 2006. Decomposing the effects of financial liberalization: Crises vs. growth. NBER working paper 12806.

Razin, Assaf, and Yona Rubinstein. 2004. *Exchange rate regimes, capital account liberalization and growth and crises: A nuanced view.* Mimeo. Tel-Aviv University.

Reinhart, Carmen M., and Christoph Trebesch. 2014. A distant mirror of debt, default, and relief. NBER working paper 20577.

Reinhart, Carmen M., and Kenneth Rogoff. 2008. Is the 2007 U.S. sub-prime financial crisis so different? An international historical comparison. NBER working paper 13761.

Reinhart, Carmen M., and M. Belen Sbrancia. 2011. The liquidation of government debt. NBER working paper 16893.

Reinhart, Carmen M., and Vincent R. Reinhart. 2010. After the fall. NBER working paper 16334.

Reinhart, Carmen, and Ken Rogoff. 2009. The aftermath of financial crises. *American Economic Review* 99 (2): 466–472.

Reis, Ricardo. 2013. The Portuguese slump and crash and the euro crisis. *Brookings Papers on Economic Activity* 46 (1): 143–210.

Rioja, Felix, Fernando Rios-Avila, and Neven Valev. 2014. The persistent effect of banking crises on investment and the role of financial markets. *Journal of Financial Economic Policy* 6 (1): 64–77.

Rivers, D., and Q. Vuong. 1988. Limited information estimators and exogeneity tests for simultaneous Probit models. *Journal of Econometrics* 39:347–366.

Rodrik, Dani, and Andres Velasco. 1999. Short-term capital flows. NBER working paper 7364 (also published in *Annual World Bank Conference on Development Economics 1999*).

Rothenberg, D. and Francis Warnock. 2006. Sudden flight and true sudden stops. NBER working paper 12726.

Saffie, Felipe E., and Sınâ T. Ates. 2013. *Fewer but better: Sudden stops, firm entry, and financial selection. Mimeo.* University of Maryland.

Sahay, Ratna, Vivek Arora, Thano Arvanities, Hamid Faruqee, Papa N'Diaye, Tommaso Mancini-Grifoli, and IMF Team. 2014. Emerging market volatility: Lessons from the Taper tantrum. IMF staff discussion note SND/14/09.

Sandleris, Guido, and Mark L. J. Wright. 2014. The costs of financial crises: Resource misallocation, productivity, and welfare in the 2001 Argentine Crisis. *Scandinavian Journal of Economics* 116 (1): 87–127.

Schmitt-Grohé, Stephanie, and Martın Uribe. 2014. Forthcoming. Downward nominal wage rigidity, currency pegs, and involuntary unemployment. *Journal of Political Economy*.

Shimer, Robert. 2012. Wage rigidities and jobless recoveries. *Journal of Monetary Economics* 59:S65–S77.

Shourideh, Ali, and Ariel Zetlin-Jones. 2012. External financing and the role of financial frictions over the business cycle: Measurement and theory. Available at SSRN 2062357.

Stockman, Alan. 1981. Anticipated inflation and the capital stock in a cash-in-advance economy. *Journal of Monetary Economics* 8:387–393.

Stokey, Nancy L. 2013. Wait-and-see: Investment options under policy uncertainty. MBER working paper 19630.

Teulings, Coen, and Richard Baldwin. 2014. *Secular Stagnation: Facts, Causes and Cures*. London: VoxEu.

Tobin, James. 1965. Money and Economic Growth. *Econometrica* 33 (4): 671–684.

Tsiang, S. C. 1980. Keynes's "finance" demand for liquidity, Robertson's loanable funds theory, and Friedman's monetarism. *Quarterly Journal of Economics* 94 (3): 467–491.

Turner, Adair. 2015. *Between Debt and the Devil: Money, Credit and Fixing Global Finance*. Princeton: Princeton University Press.

Turner, Philip. 2013. The global long-term interest rate, financial risks and policy choices in EMEs. Presented before Inter-American Development Bank's 38th Meeting of Chief Economists of Central Banks and Finance Ministries.

Woodford, Michael. 1990. Public debt as private liquidity. *American Economic Review* 80 (2): 382–388.

Woodford, Michael. 1995. Price level determinacy without control of a monetary aggregate. *Carnegie-Rochester Conference Series on Public Policy* 43 (3): 1–46.

Woodford, Michael. 2003. *Interest and Prices: Foundations of a Theory of Monetary Policy.* Princeton: Princeton University Press.

Woodford, Michael. 2009. How important is money in the conduct of monetary policy? *Journal of Money, Credit and Banking* 40 (8): 1561–1598.

Wooldridge, Jeffrey M. 2002. *Econometric Analysis of Cross Section and Panel Data.* Cambridge: MIT Press.

Index